·GLOVEBOX ATLAS·
FRANCE
AND BENELUX

Reprinted January 1993
2nd edition November 1992
1st edition March 1991
Reprinted October 1992
© The Automobile Association 1992

Produced by the Publishing Division of
The Automobile Association

Mapping produced by the Cartographic Department of
The Automobile Association.

Published by The Automobile Association, Fanum House,
Basingstoke, Hampshire RG21 2EA.

ISBN 0 7495 0665 2, ISBN 0 7495 0666 0

Printed by Graficromo SA, Cordoba, Spain

The contents of this atlas are believed correct at the time
of printing, although the publishers cannot accept any
responsibility for errors or omissions, or for changes in
the details given. They would welcome information to help
keep this atlas up to date; please write to the
Cartographic Editor, Publishing Division,
The Automobile Association, Fanum House, Basing View,
Basingstoke, Hampshire RG21 2EA.

A CIP catalogue record for this book is available from the
British Library.

Contents

Driving in France and the Low Countries
IV

Journey planning map
X

Map pages
XII

Map symbols
1

Road atlas – Benelux
2

Road atlas – France
10

Index and city plans
45

Distance Chart
84

City plans included within index

Amsterdam • Antwerpen • Bordeaux • Brugge • Bruxelles • Den Haag • Lille
• Luxembourg • Lyon • Marseille • Nice • Paris • Rotterdam • Strasbourg

Driving in France and the Low Countries

Introduction

Motoring laws in France and Benelux are just as wide-ranging and complicated as those in the UK, but they should cause little difficulty to the average British motorist. Regulations are given for each of the countries featured in this atlas. (Motoring regulations in Monaco are generally the same as in France. However, although caravans are permitted to pass through the principality, they are not permitted to stop or park.)

The AIT

The AIT is the international association of motoring clubs, to which the AA and its sister clubs are affiliated. Many offer reciprocal arrangements to members travelling abroad.

In **France** and **Monaco** the AA is affiliated to the Automobile Club National (ACN), 9 rue Anatole-de-la-Forge, F-75017 Paris *tel*: 42278200.

The Touring Club Royal de Belgique (TCB) in **Belgium** has its head office at 1040 Bruxelles, 44 rue de la Loi, Bruxelles *tel*: (02) 2332211. It is open weekdays 08.30-17.30 hours; Saturday 09.00-12.00 hours. There are branches in most towns. These are open weekdays 09.00-12.30 hrs (Mon from 09.30) and 14.00-18.00 hrs; Saturday 09.00-12.00 hrs. All offices are closed on Saturday afternoons and Sundays.

The Automobile Club du Grand-Duché de Luxembourg (ACL) has its head office at 54 route de Longwy, **Luxembourg** *tel*: 450045. Office hours are 08.30-12.00 hrs and 13.30-18.00 hrs from Monday to Friday; closed Saturdays and Sundays.

The Koninklijke Nederlandse Toeristenbond (ANWB) in the **Netherlands** has its headquarters at 2596 EC's Gravenhage, Wassenaarseweg 220 *tel*: (070) 3147714. The club has offices in most provincial towns. Offices are usually open between 08.45 and 16.45 hrs Monday to Friday and 08.45 and 12.00 hrs on Saturdays.

Breakdowns

You are advised to seek local assistance as, at the present time, there is no road assistance service provided by a member club in **France**. The use of a warning triangle or hazard warning lights is obligatory in the event of an accident or breakdown. It is recommended that a warning

riangle is always carried. The triangle must be placed on the road 30 metres (33 yards) behind the vehicle and clearly visible from 100 metres 110 yards). Note — if your vehicle is equipped with hazard warning ights, it is also compulsory to use them if you are forced to drive emporarily at a greatly reduced speed to warn approaching traffic.

The **Belgian** motoring club (TCB) maintains an efficient 24-hour preakdown service known as Touring Secours/Touring Wegenhulp. The Flemish Automobile Club (VAB-VTB), which operates in the Flemish area only, and the Royal Automobile Club of Belgium (RACB) have patrol cars displaying the signs 'Wacht op de Weg' or 'RACB', but as neither is affiliated to the AA, motorists would have to pay for their services. The use of a warning triangle is obligatory in the event of a breakdown or accident. The triangle must be placed 30 metres (33 yards) behind the vehicle on ordinary roads and 100 metres (110 yards) on motorways. It must be visible for a distance of 50 metres (55 yards).

The Automobile Club du Grand-Duché de **Luxembourg** (ACL) operates a 24-hour road assistance service throughout the whole country. The vehicles of the ACL are yellow with a black inscription '*Automobile Club Service Routier*'. This service should not be confused with the *Depannages Secours Automobiles*' (DSA), which is a commercial enterprise and not connected with the AA or any other organisation. The use of a warning triangle is compulsory in the event of an accident or breakdown. The triangle must be placed on the road about 100 metres 110 yards) behind the vehicle to warn following traffic of any obstruction.

The ANWB maintains a 24-hour road patrol service (*Wegenwacht*) which operates throughout the **Netherlands**. In the event of a breakdown or an accident a motorist must use either a warning triangle or hazard warning lights to warn approaching traffic of any obstruction. A warning triangle is recommended.

Accidents

France — **Fire** *tel*: 18. **Police** *tel*: 17. **Ambulance**, use the number given in the telephone box or, if not given, call the police (*brigade de gendarmerie*). If you are involved in an accident you must complete a *constat a l'amiable* before the vehicle is moved. This represents the European Accident Statement Form, and must be signed by the other party. In the event of a dispute and a refusal to complete the form, you should immediately obtain a *constat d'huissier*. This is a written report from a bailiff (*huissier*). A bailiff can usually be found in any large town and will charge a fee of *Fr*400 for preparing the report. The police are only called out to accidents when someone is injured, a driver is under the influence of alcohol, or if the accident impedes the traffic flow. When attending an accident the police prepare a report known as a *proces verbal*. The French authorities, at their discretion, may request a surety payment to cover the court costs or fines.

Belgium — **Fire** and **Ambulance** *tel*: 100. **Police** *tel*: 101. The police must be called if an unoccupied stationary vehicle is damaged, or if anyone is injured. If injury is involved the vehicle must not be moved.

Luxembourg — Fire *tel:* 012 — Civil Defence emergency services (*Secours d'urgence*). There are no firm rules to adopt following an accident. However, anyone requested to give assistance must do so.

Netherlands — Fire, Police, and **Ambulance** 0611. If you have a serious or complicated accident, especially if anyone is injured, the police should be called before the vehicles are moved.

Emergency Messages

Emergency messages to tourists are broadcast by **France** Inter on 1829 metres long wave, Monday to Saturday from 25 June to 31 August. The messages are transmitted in English and German after the news at 09.00 hrs and 16.00 hrs.

In **Belgium**, emergency messages to tourists are broadcast daily on Belgian Radio in French and Dutch. *Radio Television Belge* (RTBF) (483 metres medium wave) broadcasts these messages in French at 12.00 and 19.00 hrs; on 13 metres short wave at 06.00 and 17.00 hrs Monday to Friday and on 16, 19, 25, 31 and 41 metres at 17.00 hrs. *Belgische Radio en Televisie (BRT)* (198 metres medium wave) broadcasts these messages in Dutch at 12.00 and 14.00 hrs; on 16 and 19 metres short wave at 18.00 and 22.00 hrs, on 21 metres at 09.30, 12.00 and 24.00 hrs and on 31 metres (Wednesday and Saturday) and 49 metres (Monday, Tuesday, Thursday and Friday at 20.30 hrs.

In **Luxembourg**, emergency messages to tourists are broadcast during the summer on the German *RTL* programme on 208 metres medium wave, and may be given at any time between 06.00 and 01.00 hrs.

Emergency messages to tourists in the **Netherlands** are broadcast daily at 16.56 hrs on Radio 5 in Dutch on 1008 Khz medium wave at 17.55 hrs. Between 1 June and 1 October these messages are repeated every day on the same wavelength at 23.02 hrs.

How to use the Phone

In **France**, insert either a one franc coin or phonecard (Télécarte) **after** lifting the receiver to obtain a continuous dialling tone. Phonecards may be purchased from airports, post offices, railway stations and retailers displaying the sign 'Télécarte en vente ici'. Coins accepted are 50 *centimes* and *Fr*1, 5 or 10. International call boxes have metallic grey payphones. Cardphones can also be used for international calls. You can benefit from 50% extra time by making calls when the 'cheap rate' operates — weekdays between 22.30 and 08.00 hrs, weekends from 14.00 hrs on a Saturday.

Telephone codes — UK to France — 010 33
France to UK — 19 * 44
France to Republic of Ireland — 19 * 353
France to the USA — 19 * 1 (* wait for second dialling tone).

In **Belgium**, insert the coin **after** lifting the receiver. The dialling tone is the same as in the UK. Use *BFr*5 coins for local calls and *BFr*5 (*BFr*20 in some boxes) coins for national and international calls. International call boxes are identified with European flags, and a call to the UK costs *BFr*29.75 per minute. Cardphones can also be used for international calls.

Telephone codes — UK to Belgium — 010 32
　　　　　　　　Belgium to UK — 00 * 44
　　　　　　　　Belgium to Republic of Ireland — 00 * 353
　　　　　　　　Belgium to the USA — 00 * 1 (* wait for
　　　　　　　　second dialling tone).

In **Luxembourg**, insert the coin **after** lifting the receiver; the dialling tone is the same as in the UK. Use *LFr*5 coins for local calls and *LFr*5 or 20 coins for national and international calls. International call boxes are situated along roadsides. A telephone call to the UK costs *LFr*75 for three minutes and *LFr*25 for each additional minute.

Telephone codes — UK to Luxembourg — 010 352
　　　　　　　　Luxembourg to UK — 00 44
　　　　　　　　Luxembourg to Republic of Ireland — 00 353
　　　　　　　　Luxembourg to the USA — 00 1.

To use the phone in the **Netherlands**, insert the coin **after** lifting the receiver. Use 25 *cent* coins or *Fls*1.00 coins (instructions appear in English in all public call boxes). When making calls to subscribers within the Netherlands, precede the number with the relevant area code. All payphones and cardphones can be used for international phone calls. The cost of a call to the UK is *Fls*0.95 for each minute. Local calls cost 25 *cents*. The cheap rate operates daily from 18.00-08.00 hrs; the charge is *Fls*0.70 per minute for calls to the UK.

Telephone codes — UK to the Netherlands — 010 31
　　　　　　　　Netherlands to UK — 09 * 44
　　　　　　　　Netherlands to Republic of Ireland — 09 * 353
　　　　　　　　Netherlands to the USA — 09 * 1 (* wait for
　　　　　　　　second dialling tone).

Motorway Tolls

With the exception of a few sections into or around large cities, all motorways (autoroutes) in **France** have a toll charged according to the distance travelled. On the majority of toll motorways, a travel ticket is issued on entry and the toll is paid on leaving the motorway. The ticket gives all the relevant information about the toll charges, including the toll category of your vehicle. On some motorways toll collection is automatic; have the correct amount ready to throw into the collecting basket. If change is required, use the marked separate lane.

All motorways are toll-free in **Belgium** and **Luxembourg**.
Tolls are charged on some motorways in the **Netherlands.**

Speed Limits

In **France**, the beginning of a built-up area is indicated by a sign with the placename in blue letters on a light background; the end by the placename sign with a thin red line diagonally across it. Unless otherwise signposted, speed limits are:
Built-up area 50kph (31mph).
Outside built-up areas on normal roads 90kph (55mph); on dual-carriageways separated by a central reservation 110kph (68mph).
On motorways 130kph (80mph).

Unless otherwise signposted, the following speed limits apply in **Belgium:**
Car/caravan/trailer
Built-up area 50kph (31mph)
Other roads 90kph (55mph)
Motorways and 4-lane roads separated by a central reservation 120kph (74mph).

In **Luxembourg**, the placename indicates the beginning and the end of a built-up area. Unless otherwise signposted, speed limits are as follows:
Built-up areas 50kph (31mph)
Main roads 90kph (55mph)
Motorways 120kph (74mph)
Lower limits apply to caravans. All lower signposted speed limits must be adhered to.

In the **Netherlands**, the placename indicates the beginning and the end of a built-up area. Unless otherwise signposted, speed limits are as follows:
Built-up areas 50kph (31mph)
Outside built-up areas 80kph (49mph)
Motorways 120kph (74mph).

Vehicles towing a caravan or trailer are limited to 80kph (49mph).

Seat Belts

In **France, Belgium, Luxembourg** and the **Netherlands**, seat belts are compulsory, if fitted, for drivers and passengers.

Children

In **France**, children under 10 are not permitted to travel in a vehicle as a front-seat passenger unless in an approved child restraint or using a seat belt. In **Luxembourg** children under 10 are not permitted to travel in a vehicle as a front-seat passenger if rear seating is available. Children under 10 must wear a child restraint if occupying a front-seat.

Children under 12 in **Belgium** are not permitted to travel in a vehicle as a front-seat passenger except when using a special seat or when rear seats are not available or already occupied by children.

Children under 12 and under 150cms in height in the **Netherlands** are not permitted to travel in a vehicle as a front-seat passenger, unless using special baby seat or child restraint.

Currency

The unit of currency in **France** is the *franc* (*Fr*), divided into 100 *centimes*. There are no restrictions on the amount of foreign or French currency that can be taken into France. However, a declaration must be made on entry if it is likely that bank notes to a value of *Fr*50,000 or more are likely to be re-exported.

In **Belgium** the unit of currency is the *Belgian franc* (*BFr*), divided into 100 *centimes*. The unit of currency in **Luxembourg** is the *Luxembourg franc* (*LFr*), divided into 100 *centimes*. In the **Netherlands**, the unit of currency is the *Dutch gilder*, or *florin* (*Fls*), divided into 100 *cents*.

There are no restrictions on the amount of foreign or local currency that can be taken into or out of **Belgium, Luxembourg** and the **Netherlands**. However, because of the limited market for Luxembourg notes in other countries, it is advisable to change them into Belgium or other foreign notes before leaving the country.

Driving Licence

A valid UK or Republic of Ireland driving licence is acceptable in **France** and **Monaco**. The minimum age at which a visitor may use a temporarily imported car is 18 years. In France a visitor may use a temporarily imported motorcycle of up to 80cc at 16 but must be at least 18 to use one over 80cc. (In Monaco up to 125cc at 16, but 18 if over 125cc.)

A valid UK or Republic of Ireland driving licence is acceptable in **Belgium, Luxembourg** and the **Netherlands**. The minimum age at which a visitor may use a temporarily imported car or motorcycle is 18 for Belgium and the Netherlands and 17 for Luxembourg.

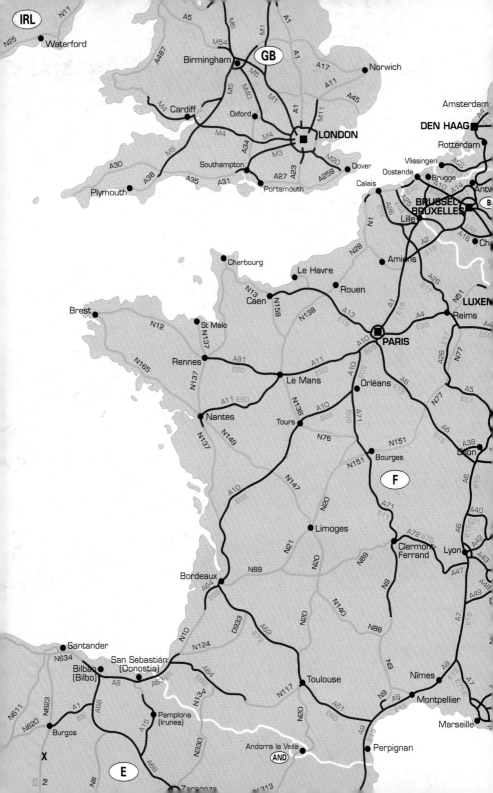

Journey planning map

Map pages

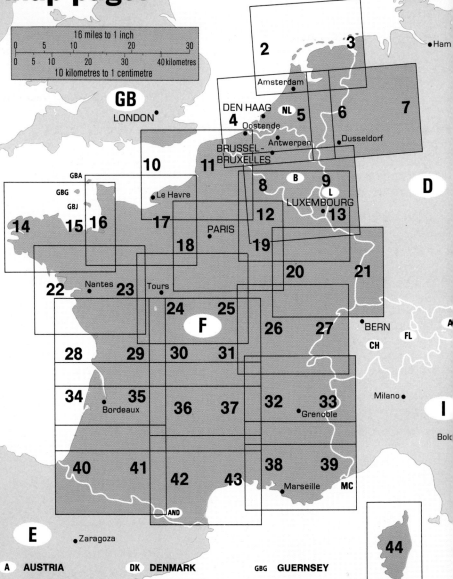

16 miles to 1 inch

0   5   10   20   30

0 5 10   20   30   40 kilometres

10 kilometres to 1 centimetre

DK

Ham

GB

LONDON

2

3

Amsterdam

DEN HAAG

NL

5

6

7

4

Oostende

Dusseldorf

BRUSSEL-
BRUXELLES

Antwerpen

D

10

11

8

B

9

L

Le Havre

LUXEMBOURG

GBA

12

13

GBG

GBJ

17

19

14

15

16

PARIS

18

20

21

22

Nantes

23

Tours

24

25

BERN

F

26

27

FL

CH

A

28

29

30

31

32

33

Milano

34

35

36

37

Grenoble

I

Bordeaux

40

41

42

43

38

39

Bol

AND

Marseille

MC

E

Zaragoza

44

A AUSTRIA	**DK** DENMARK	**GBG** GUERNSEY
AND ANDORRA	**E** SPAIN	**GBJ** JERSEY
B BELGIUM	**F** FRANCE	**I** ITALY
CH SWITZERLAND	**FL** LIECHTENSTEIN	**L** LUXEMBOURG
D FEDERAL REPUBLIC OF GERMANY	**GB** UNITED KINGDOM	**MC** MONACO
	GBA ALDERNEY	**NL** NETHERLANDS

XII

Map symbols

[A4]	Motorway - dual carriageway
[A7]	Motorway - single carriageway
[A1]	Toll motorway - dual carriageway
[A6]	Toll motorway - single carriageway
	Motorway junction
	Motorway junction - restricted access
	Motorway service area
	Motorway under construction
	Primary route
	Main road
	Secondary road
	Other road
D600 [E57] N59	Road numbers
	Dual carriageway or four lanes
	Road in poor condition
	Scotland: narrow A roads with passing places
	Under construction
[TOLL] Toll	Toll road
	Transit route (G.D.R)
	Scenic route
)========(	Road tunnel
	Car transporter (rail)

68	Distances (distances in GB & Ireland are in miles elsewhere in Europe in kilometres)
10·6 970	Mountain pass (height in metres) with closure period
	Gradient 14% and over. Arrow points uphill
	Gradient 6% - 13% Gradient 20% and over in G.B.
	Frontier crossing with restricted opening hours
	Frontier posts
AA	AA shop
AA	AA port shop
IBIZA	Vehicle ferry
	Hovercraft ferry
	Airport
	International boundary
	National boundary
	Viewpoint
	Motor racing circuit
3560 SNOWDON	Mountain/spot height (heights in G.B. and Ireland in feet elsewhere in Europe in metres)
	Mountain railway
	Urban area
	River, lake and canal
■ Kukkola Rapids	Place of interest
8	Overlaps and numbers of continuing pages

1

A   B   C

4

3

West-Terschelling   Te

Vlieland

De Cocksdorp

De Koog

Den Burg

Texel   **Afsluitdijk**

E22

A7

Den Helder

Den Oever

De Kooy   N99

Staver

Anna Paulowna   A7

N249   *Ijssel*

N248

Schagen   *Medemblik*

N242   *Andijk*

Bergen   *Hoogkarspel* *En*

Bergen aan Zee N242   N3

Egmond aan Zee **Alkmaar** N7

N243 *Huizen* *Hoorn*

E19

A9   N244 A7   **Markerwaard**

Castricum   N241

Purmerend *Edam*

Beverwijk N8 *Wormerveer* *Volendam*

NATIONAAL PARK DE **Ijmuiden**

KENNEMER DUINEN **Zaandam** *Monnickendam*

HAARLEM

Zandvoort **AMSTERDAM** *Almere*

Heemstede A9   A6

Hillegom A1 N27

A4   A9 *Huizen*

Noordwijk aan Zee *Lisse* *Aalsmeer* *Naarden* E231

N208 *Sassenheim* A2 *Bussum*

Katwijk aan Zee A44 *Uithoorn* *Spakenburg*

E19 N201 *Baarn*

4 E35 **Hilversum**

Wassenaar **Leiden** N207 *Soestdijk*

Noord Hollands Duin Reservaat

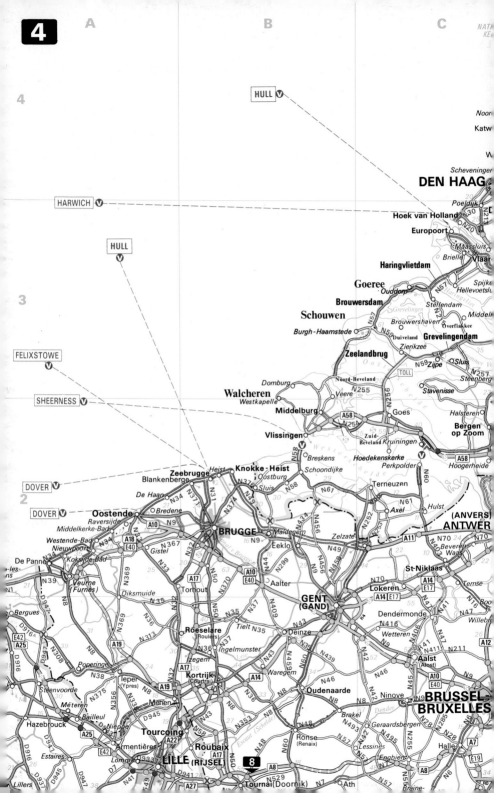

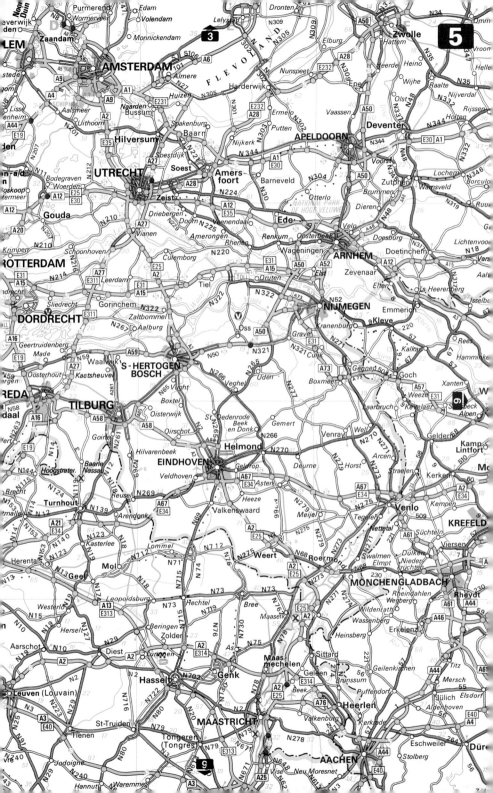

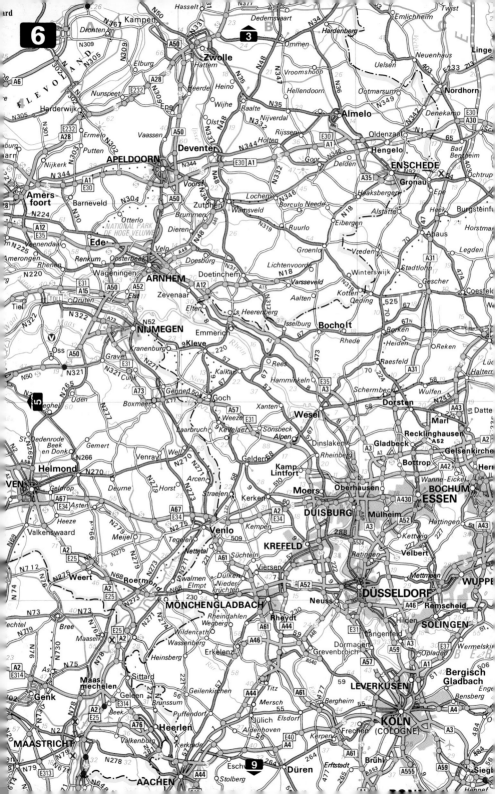

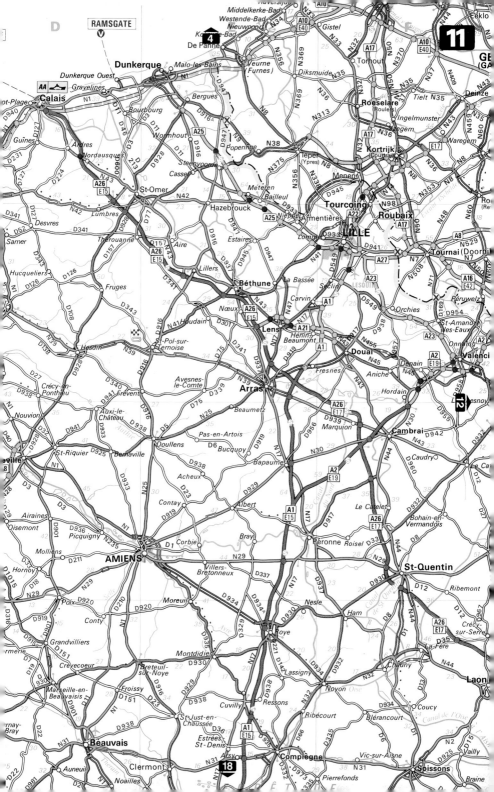

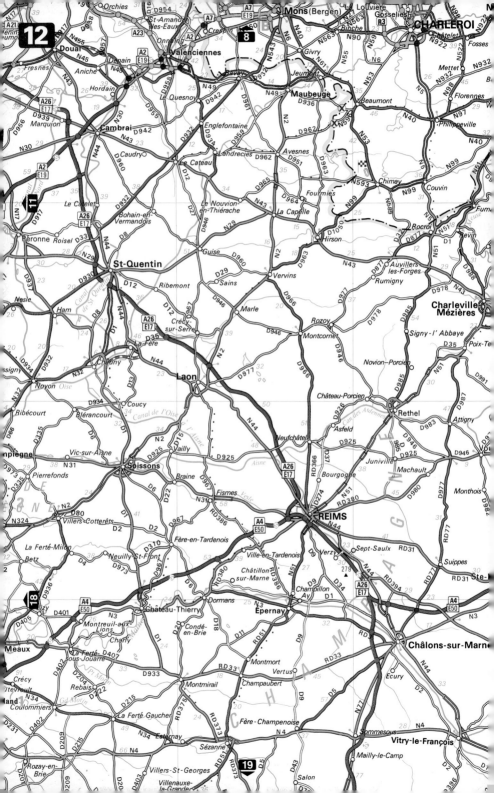

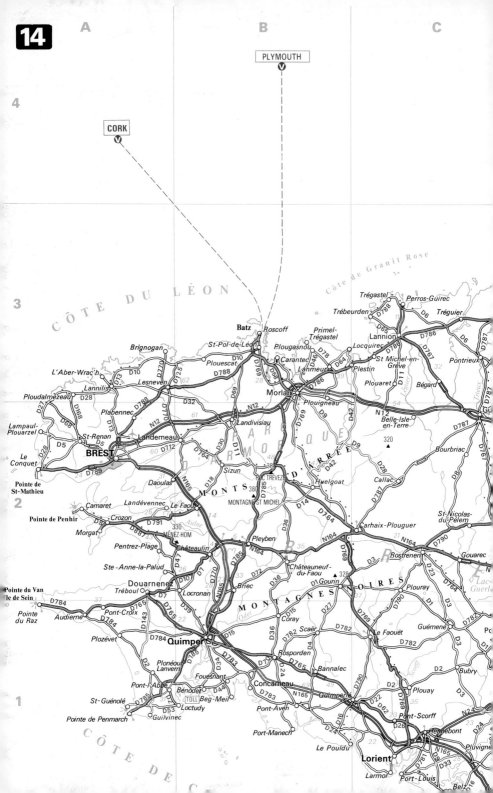

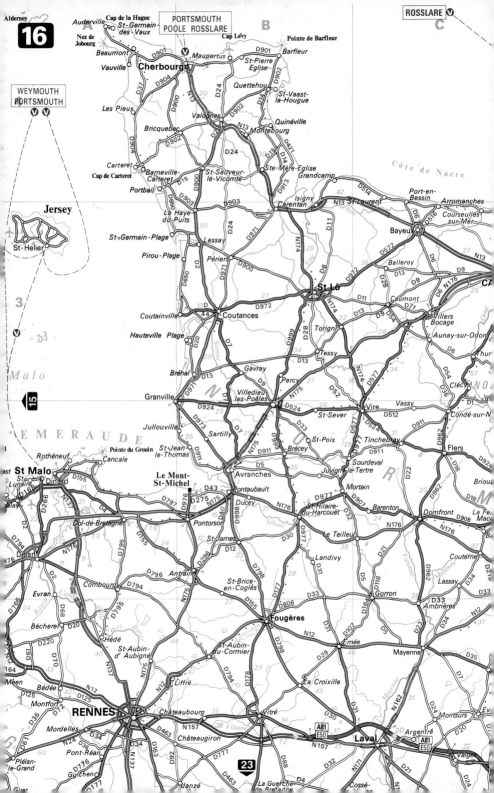

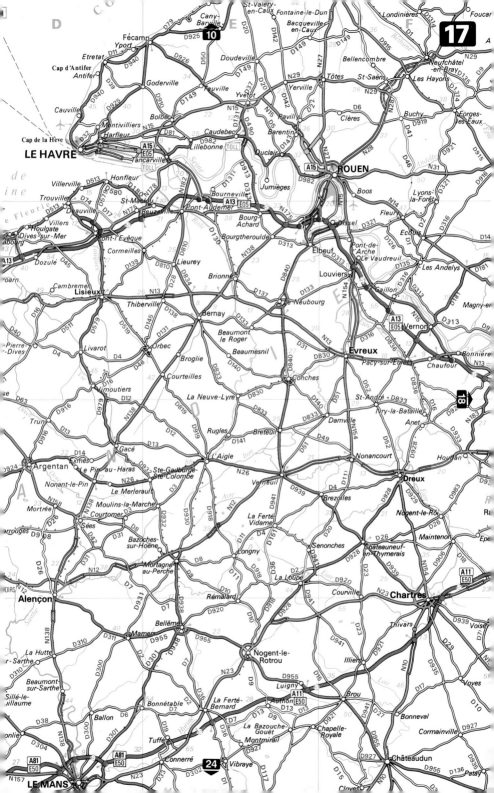

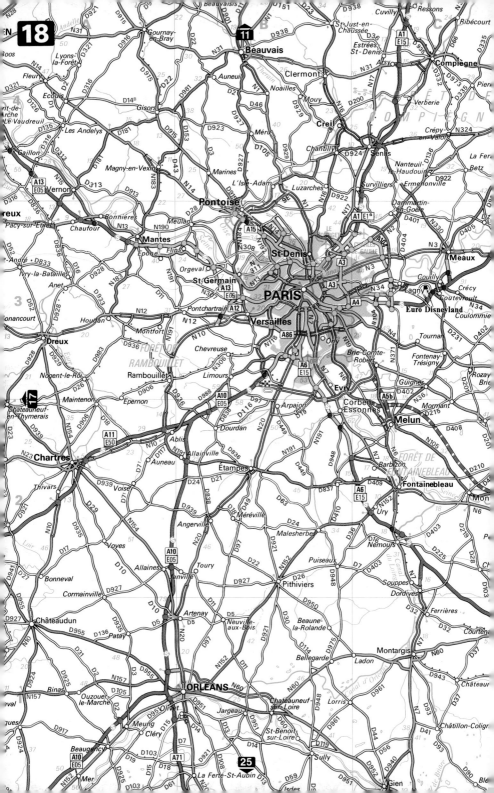

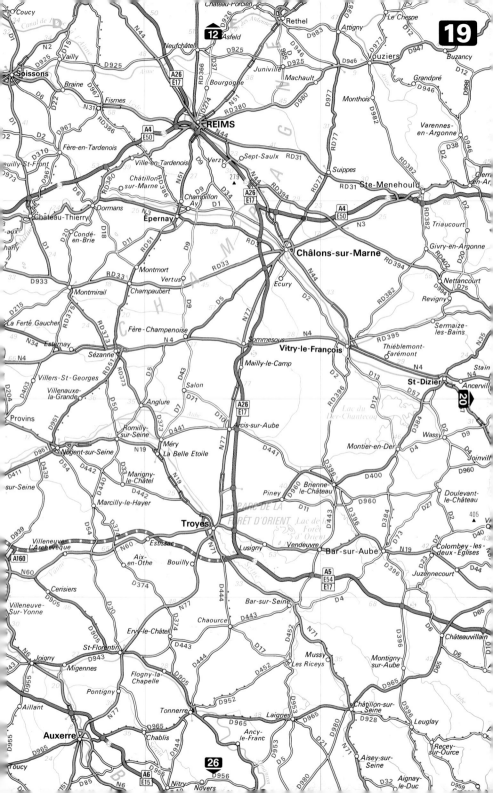

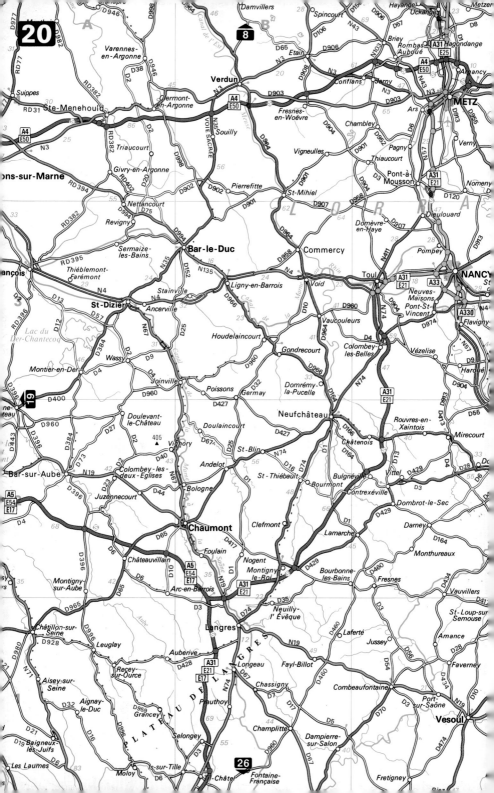

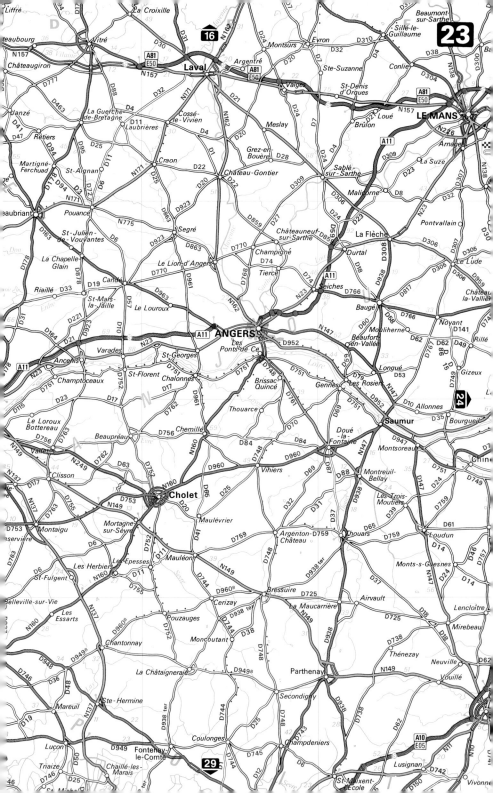

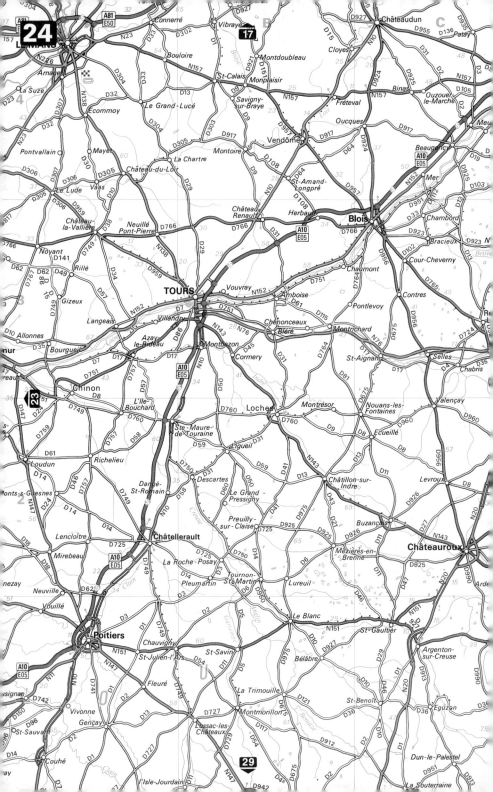

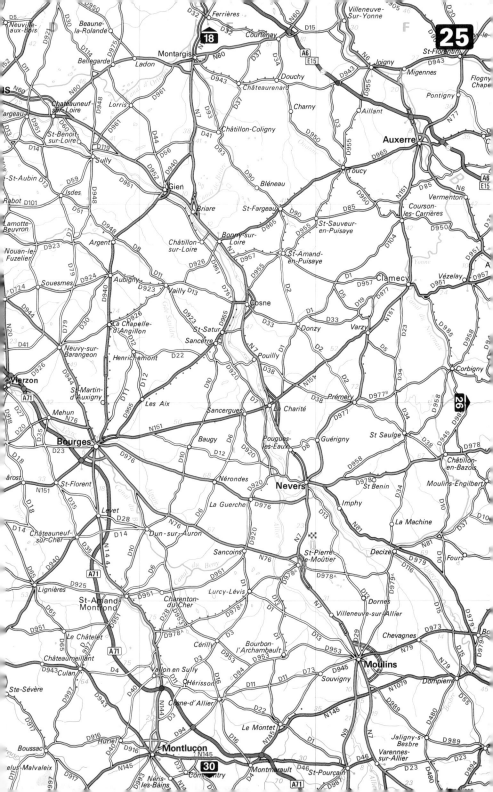

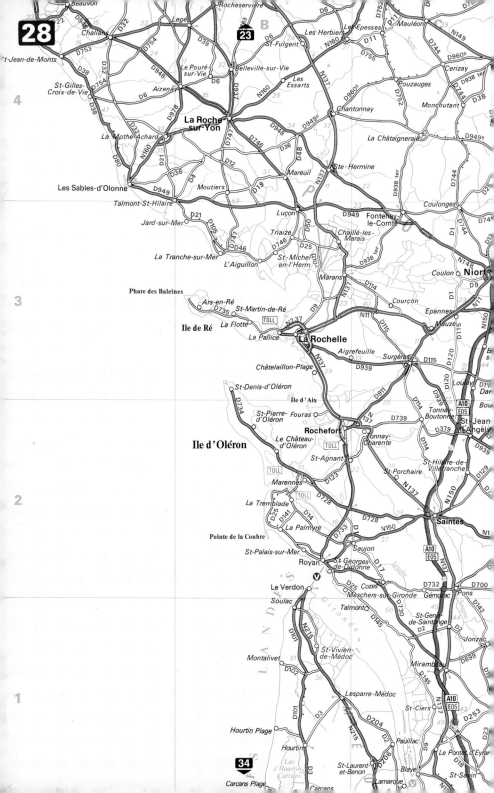

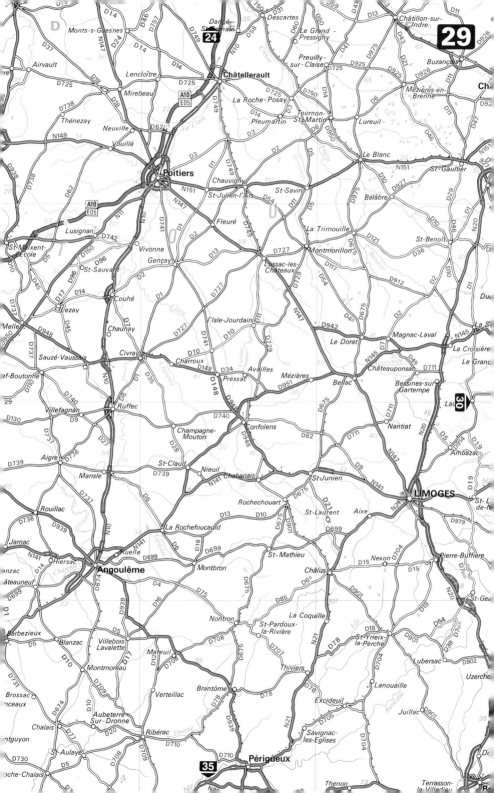

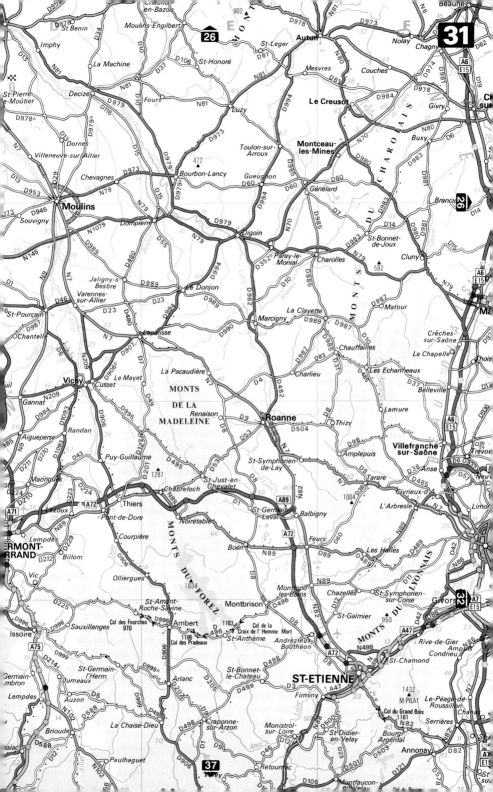

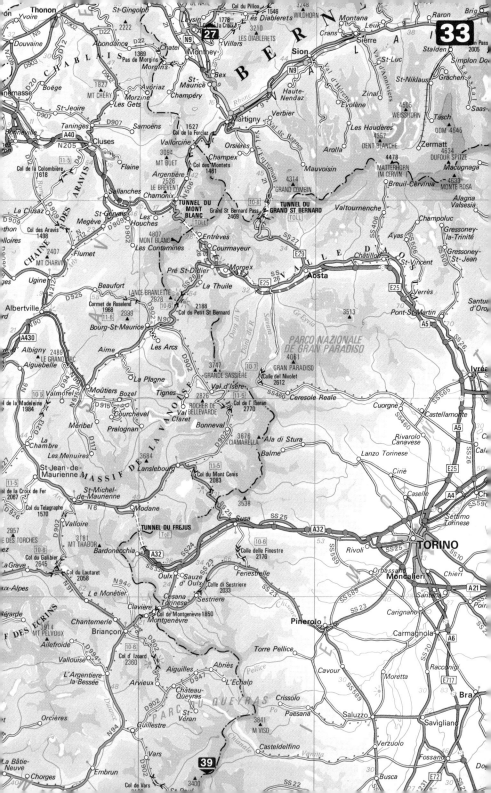

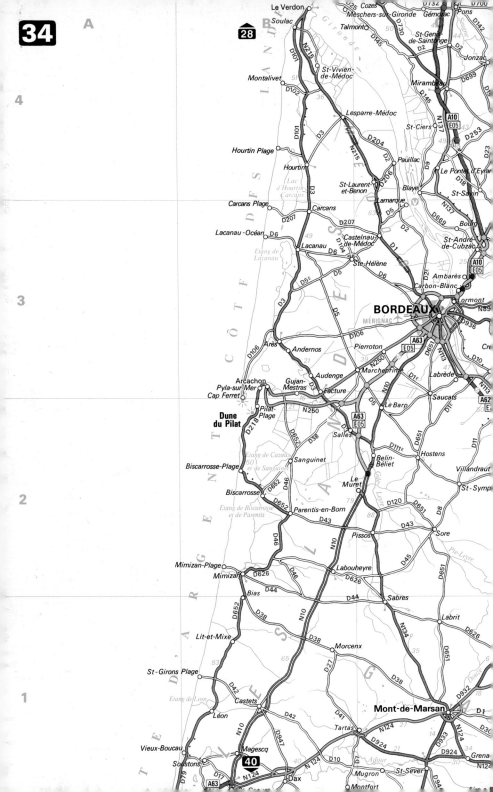

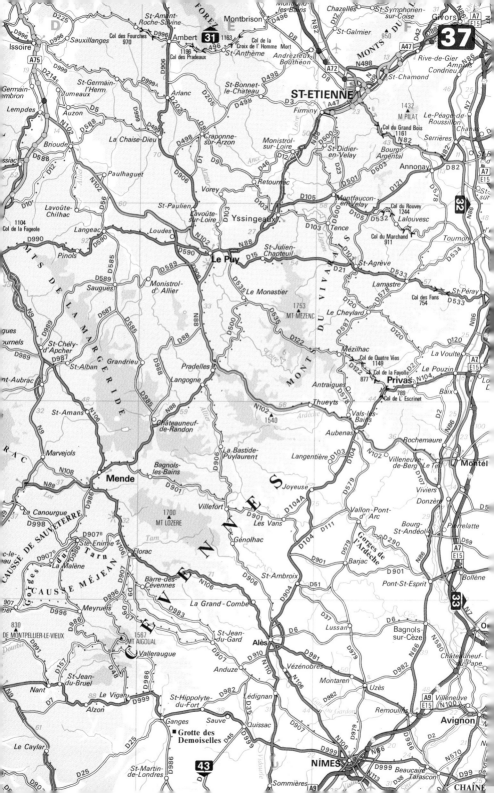

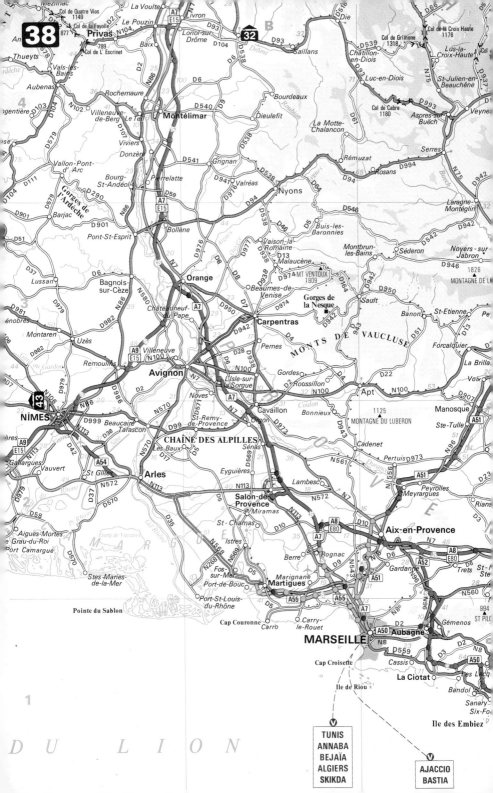

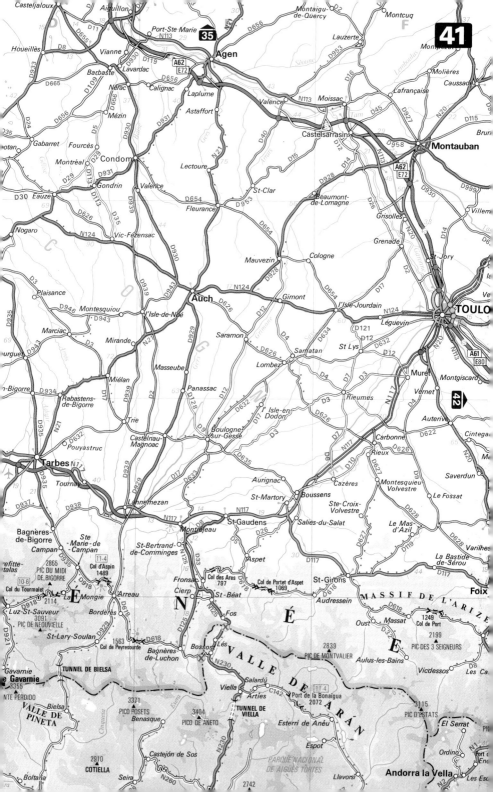

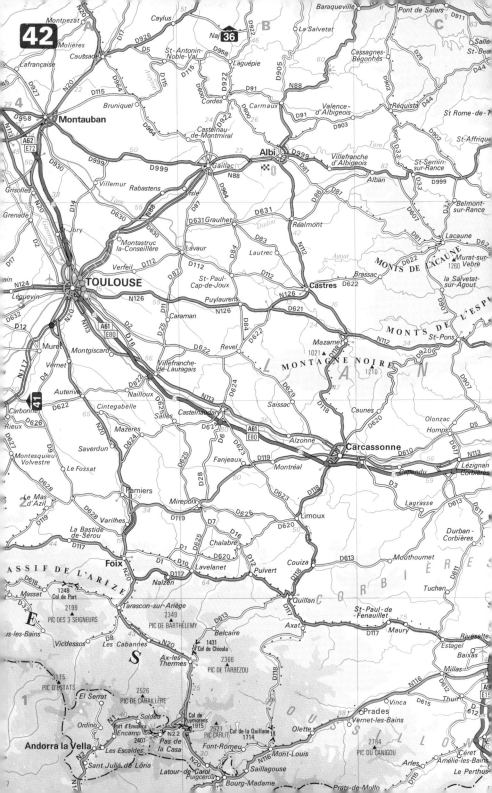

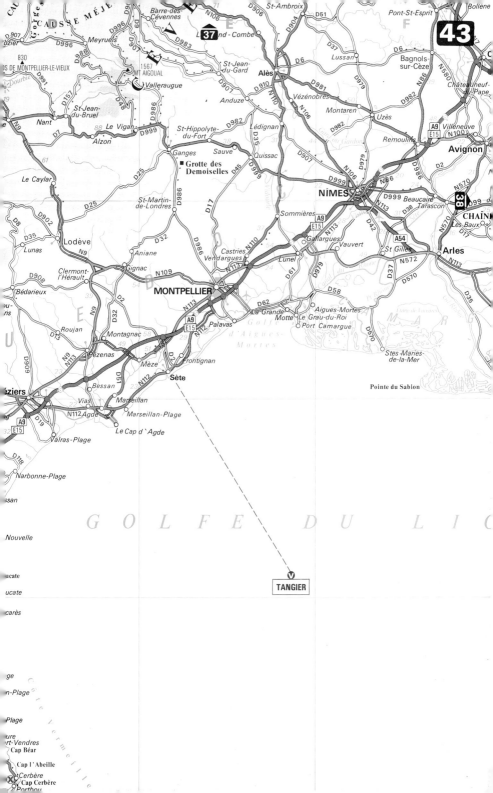

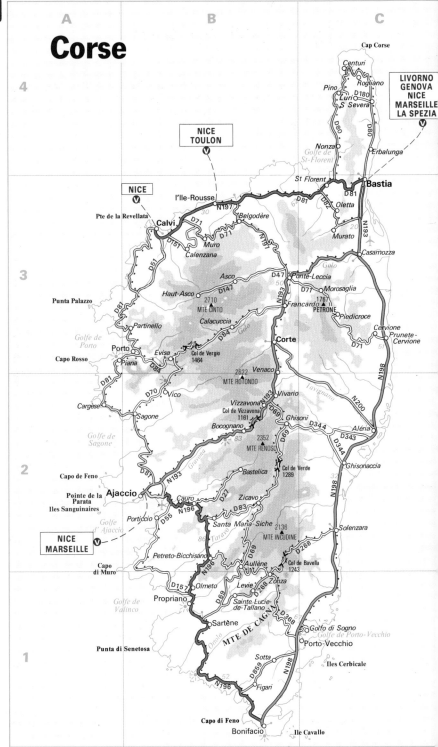

44

Corse

A   B   C

4

3

2

1

Cap Corse

Centuri
Rogliano
Pino
D 180
Luri
S Severa

NICE
TOULON

Nonza
Golfe de
St-Florent
Erbalunga

NICE

St Florent
Bastia
D 81
Oletta
D 82

I'lle-Rousse
N 197
Murato
N 193
Casamozza

Pte de la Revellata
Calvi
D 71
Belgodère
Muro
D 71
Calenzana
D 151
N 191

D 51
Asco
D 47
Ponte-Leccia
Haut-Asco
D 147
D 71
Morosaglia
Punta Palazzo
2710
1767
MTE CINTO
Francardo
PETRONE
D 81
Calacuccia
N 193
Piedicroce
Partinello
Cervione
Corte
Prunete-
Cervione
Golfe de
Porto
Evisa
Col de Vergio
1464
D 84
D 71
Porto
Piana
Venaco
N 198
Capo Rosso
D 81
2622
MTE ROTONDO
D 70
Vico
Vivario
Tavignano
Cargèse
Vizzavona
N 193
Sagone
Col de Vizzavona
1161
D 69
Ghisoni
N 200
Bocognano
D 344
Aléria
Golfe de
Sagone
2352
D 69
D 343
MTE RENOSO

Capo de Feno
D 81
N 193
Bastelica
Col de Verde
1289
Ghisonaccia

Pointe de la
Parata
Iles Sanguinaires
Ajaccio
Cauro
D 27
Zicavo
N 198
Porticcio
D 55
N 196
D 83
Santa Maria-Siche
2136
MTE INCUDINE
Solenzara
Golfe
d'Ajaccio
Tavaro
D 69

NICE
MARSEILLE
Petreto-Bicchisano
Aullène
Col de Bavella
1243
Capo
di Muro
D 157
Olmeto
Levie
Zonza
D 268
Propriano
D 69
Sainte Lucie-
de-Tallano
D 368
Sartène
MTE DE CAGNA
Golfe di Sogno
Golfe de
Valinco
Golfe de Porto-Vecchio
Porto-Vecchio

Punta di Senetosa
Onolo
Sotta
Iles Cerbicale
N 198

D 859
Figari

N 196

Capo di Feno

Bonifacio
Ile Cavallo

LIVORNO
GENOVA
NICE
MARSEILLE
LA SPEZIA

Index to place names

To locate a place in the atlas first look up the name in the alphabetical index. The required page number is indicated in bold type. The letter and figure in light type relate to the grid square containing the place on the atlas page. The placename is then found between the intersection of the lines linking the letters (running top and bottom of the page) and the numbers (at the left/right hand-side of the page).

City plans included within the index

Amsterdam	46/47
Antwerpen	48/49
Bordeaux	50/51
Brugge	52
Bruxelles	54/55
Den Haag	56/57
Lille	64/65
Luxembourg	66/67
Lyon	68/69
Marseille	70/71
Nice	72/73
Paris	74/75
Rotterdam	76/77
Strasbourg	78/79

A

Aalburg	5	E3
Aalsmeer	5	D4
Aalst (Alost)	4	C1
Aalten	6	B3
Aalter	4	B2
Aarschot	5	D1
Abbeville	11	D2
Ablis	18	A2
Abondance	27	F1
Abreschviller	21	D3
Abries	33	E1
Accous	40	C2
Acheux	11	E2
Agay	39	E2
Agde	43	D2
Agen	35	E2
Ahun	30	B2
Aignay-le-Duc	26	B4
Aigre	29	D2
Aigrefeuille	28	C3
Aigrefeuille-Sur-Maine	23	D2
Aiguebelle	33	D3
Aiguebelle	39	D1
Aigueperse	31	D2
Aigues-Mortes	43	E3
Aiguilles	33	E1
Aiguillon	35	D2
Aigurande	30	B3
Ailefroide	33	D1
Aillant	25	F4
Aime	33	D3
Ainhoa	40	A2
Airaines	11	D2
Aire	11	E3
Aire-sur-l'Adour	40	C3
Airvault	23	F1
Aisey-sur-Seine	26	B4
Aissey	27	E3
Aisy-sur-Armançon	26	B4
Aixe	29	F2
Aix-en-Othe	19	D2
Aix-en-Provence	38	C2
Aix-les-Bains	32	C3
Aizenay	22	C1
Ajaccio	44	B2
Alban	42	C4
Albens	32	C3
Albert	11	E2
Albertville	33	D3
Albi	42	B4
Alençon	17	D2
Aléria	44	C2
Alès	37	E1
Alkmaar	2	B2
Allaines	18	A2

45

Allainville

Allainville ....18......B2
Allanche ....36......C4
Allemond ....32......C2
Allevard ....32......C2
Allonnes ....23......F2
Allos ....39......D3
Almelo ....6......B4
Almere ....2......C1
Alost (Aalst) ....4......C1
Alphen-ann-de-Rijn ....5......D4
Altkirch ....21......E1
Alvignac ....36......A3
Alzon ....43......D4
Alzonne ....42......B2
Amance ....20......C1
Amancey ....27......D3
Amay ....9......D4
Ambarès ....34......C3
Ambazac ....30......A2
Ambérieu-en-Bugey ....32......B4
Ambert ....31......E1
Amboise ....24......B3
Ambrières ....16......C1
Amélie-les-Bains ....42......C1
Amerongen ....5......E3
Amersfoort ....5......E4
Amiens ....11......E2
Amou ....40......C3
Amphion ....27......E1
Amplepuis ....31......F2
Ampuis ....32......A2
Amsterdam ....2......C1
Ancenis ....23......D3
Ancerville ....20......A3
Ancy-le-Franc ....26......A4
Andelot ....20......B2
Andenne ....8......C3
Andernos ....34......B3
Andijk ....2......C2
Andolsheim ....21......E2
Andrézieux-Bouthéon ....31......E1
Anduze ....37......E1
Anet ....18......A3
Angers ....23......E3
Angerville ....18......B2
Anglet ....40......A3
Anglure ....19......D2
Angoulême ....29......D2
Aniane ....43......D3
Aniche ....12......A4
Anjum ....3......D3
Anna Paulowna ....2......B2
Annecy ....32......C3
Annemasse ....33......D4
Annonay ....32......A2
Annot ....39......E3
Anse ....32......A3
Anseremme ....8......C3
Anthéor ....39......E2
Antibes ....39......E2
Antifer ....10......A1
Antraigues ....37......F3
Antrain ....16......B2
Antwerpen (Anvers) ....4......C2
Anvers (Antwerpen) ....4......C2
Apeldoorn ....6......A4
Appingedam ....3......E3
Apt ....38......C3
Arachon ....34......B3
Aramits ....40......C2
Arbois ....27......D2
Arcen ....5......F2

Arc-en-Barrois ....20......A2
Arches ....21......D2
Archiac ....28......C1
Arcis-sur-Aube ....19......E2
Ardentes ....24......C2
Ardres ....11......D4
Arendonk ....5......D2
Ares ....34......B3
Argancy ....13......F2
Argelès-Gazost ....41......D2

Argelès-Plage

Argelès-Plage	**43**	D1	Arlanc	**31**	E1
Argelès-sur-Mer	**42**	C1	Arles	**42**	C1
Argent	**25**	D3	Arles	**38**	A2
Argentan	**17**	D2	Arlon	**9**	D2
Argentat	**36**	B3	Armentières	**11**	E3
Argentière	**33**	E4	Arnage	**24**	A4
Argenton-Château	**23**	E2	Arnay-le-Duc	**26**	B3
Argenton-sur-Creuse	**30**	A4	Arnhem	**6**	A3
Argentré	**23**	E4	Arpajon	**18**	B2
Arinthod	**27**	D1	Arracourt	**21**	D3

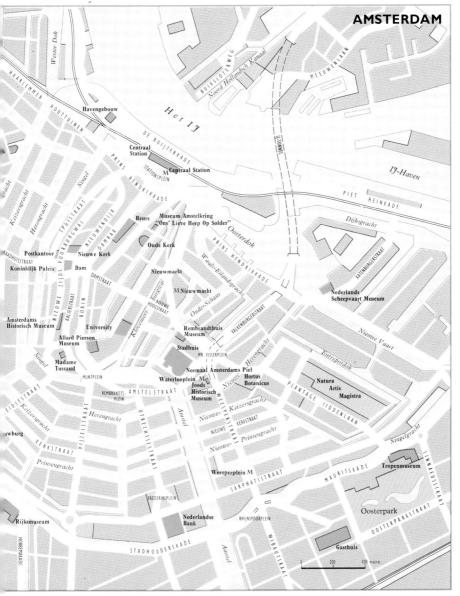

AMSTERDAM

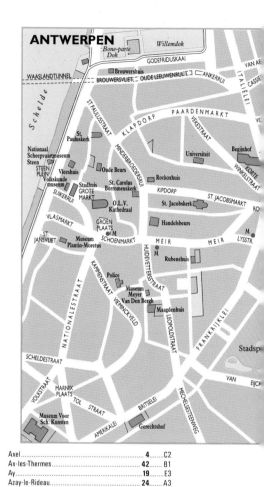

B

48

Balbigny

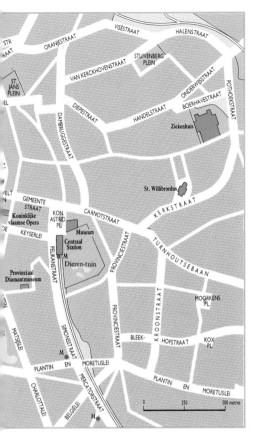

Balbigny	**31**	E2
Balleroy	**16**	C3
Ballon	**17**	D1
Bandol	**38**	C1
Bangor	**22**	A3
Bannalec	**14**	B1
Banon	**38**	C3
Banyuls	**43**	D1
Bapaume	**11**	E2
Baraqueville	**36**	C2
Barbaste	**35**	D1
Barbezieux	**29**	D1
Barbizon	**18**	C2
Barbotan	**41**	D4
Barcelonnette	**39**	E4
Barentin	**17**	E4
Barenton	**16**	C2
Barfleur	**16**	B4
Barjac	**37**	F2
Barjols	**39**	D2
Bar-le-Duc	**20**	B3
Barneveld	**5**	E4
Barneville-Carteret	**16**	A4
Barr	**21**	E3
Barre-des-Cévennes	**37**	E2
Barrême	**39**	D3
Bar-sur-Aube	**19**	F2
Bar-sur-Seine	**19**	E1

Bastelica	**44**	B2
Bastia	**44**	C4
Bastogne	**9**	D2
Battice	**9**	D4
Batz	**22**	B3
Baud	**22**	A4
Baugé	**23**	F3
Baugy	**25**	E2
Baume-les-Dames	**27**	E3
Bavay	**12**	B4
Bayeux	**16**	C3
Bayon	**20**	C3
Bayonne	**40**	A3
Bazas	**35**	D2
Bazoches-sur-Hoëne	**17**	E2
Beaucaire	**38**	A2
Beaufort	**33**	D3
Beaufort-en-Vallée	**23**	F3
Beaugency	**24**	C4
Beaulieu	**39**	F2
Beaulieu-sur-Dordogne	**36**	B3
Beaumes-de-Venise	**38**	B3
Beaumesnil	**17**	E3
Beaumetz	**11**	E2
Beaumont	**16**	A4
Beaumont	**35**	E3
Beaumont	**8**	B3
Beaumont-de-Lomagne	**41**	F4
Beaumont le Roger	**17**	E3
Beaumont-sur-Sarthe	**17**	D1
Beaune	**26**	C3
Beaune-la-Rolande	**18**	B1
Beaupréau	**23**	D2
Beauraing	**8**	C3
Beaurepaire	**32**	B2
Beaurepaire-en-Bresse	**26**	C2
Beauvais	**11**	D1
Beauvallon	**39**	E1
Beauvezer	**39**	D3
Beauvoir	**22**	C2
Beauvoir-sur-Niort	**28**	C3
Bécherel	**15**	E2
Bédarieux	**43**	D3
Bédée	**15**	E1
Bedous	**40**	C2
Beek	**5**	E1
Beek en Donk	**5**	E2
Bégard	**14**	C3
Beg-Meil	**14**	B1
Beilen	**3**	E2
Bélâbre	**29**	F4
Belcaire	**42**	B1
Belfort	**27**	F4
Belgodère	**44**	B3
Belin-Béliet	**34**	C2
Bellac	**29**	F3
Bellegarde	**18**	B1
Bellegarde	**32**	C4
Bellegarde-en-Marche	**30**	B2
Belle-Isle-en-Terre	**14**	C2
Bellême	**17**	E1
Bellencombre	**10**	C1
Belleville	**32**	A4
Belleville-sur-Vie	**23**	D1
Belley	**32**	C3
Belmont-sur-Rance	**42**	C4
Belœil	**8**	A4
Belvès	**35**	F3
Belz	**22**	A4
Bénévent l'Abbaye	**30**	A3
Benfeld	**21**	E3
Bénodet	**14**	B1

Berck-Plage	10	C3
Bergen (Mons)	8	B3
Bergen	2	B2
Bergen aan Zee	2	B2
Bergen op Zoom	4	C2
Bergerac	35	E3
Bergues	11	E4
Bergum	3	D3
Beringen	5	E1
Bernaville	11	D2
Bernay	17	E3
Berres	38	B2
Bertrix	8	C2
Besançon	27	D3
Bessan	43	D3
Besse-en-Chandesse	30	C1
Besse-sur-Issole	39	D2
Bessines-sur-Gartempe	30	A3
Béthune	11	E3
Betz	18	C4
Beuil	39	E3
Beuzeville	17	D3
Beveren-Waas	4	C2
Beverwijk	2	B1
Beynac-et-Cazenac	35	F3
Beynat	36	A3
Béziers	43	D3
Biarritz	40	A3
Bias	34	B2
Bidache	40	B3
Bidart	40	A3
Bierre-Lès-Semur	26	B3
Billom	31	D2
Binas	18	A1
Binche	8	B3
Binic	15	D2
Biscarrosse	34	B2
Biscarrosse-Plage	34	B2
Bitche	21	E4
Blain	22	C3
Blâmont	21	D3
Blangy	11	D2
Blankenberge	4	B2
Blanzac	29	D1
Blaye	34	C4
Bléneau	25	E4
Blérancourt	11	F1
Bléré	24	B3
Blériot-Plage	11	D4
Bletterans	27	D2
Bligny	26	B3
Blois	24	C3
Blokzijl	3	D2
Bocognano	44	B2
Bodegraven	5	D4
Boëge	27	E1
Boën	31	E2
Bohain-en-Vermandois	12	A3
Bolbec	10	B1
Bollène	38	A3
Bologne	20	B2
Bolsward	3	D2
Bonifacio	44	B1
Bonlieu	27	D2
Bonnat	30	B3
Bonnétable	17	D1
Bonneval	17	F1
Bonneval	33	E2
Bonneville	33	D4
Bonnières	18	A3
Bonnieux	38	B2
Bonny-sur-Loire	25	E3
Boom	4	C1
Boos	17	F4
Borculo	6	B3
Bordeaux	34	C3
Bordères	41	D1
Borger	3	E2
Bormes-les-Mimosas	39	D1
Bort-les-Orgues	30	C1
Boskoop	5	D4
Bouaye	22	C2
Bouillon	8	C2
Bouilly	19	E2
Boulay-Moselle	13	F2
Boulogne-sur-Gesse	41	E2
Boulogne-sur-Mer	11	D4
Bouloire	24	A4
Bourbon Lancy	26	A2
Bourbon-l'Archambault	31	D4

BORDEAUX

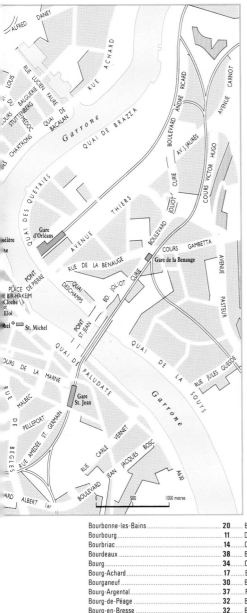

Bourgtheroulde .... **17** E3
Bourgueil .... **24** A3
Bourmont .... **20** B2
Bourneville .... **17** E4
Boussac .... **30** B3
Boussens .... **41** E2
Bouvignes .... **8** C3
Bouvron .... **22** C3
Bouxwiller .... **21** E4
Bouzonville .... **13** F2
Boxmeer .... **5** F3
Boxtel .... **5** E2
Bozel .... **33** D3
Bracieux .... **24** C3
Braine .... **12** A2
Braine-le-Comte .... **8** B4
Brakel .... **4** B1
Brancion .... **26** B2
Branne .... **35** D3
Brantôme .... **35** E4
Brassac .... **42** C3
Brasschaat .... **5** D2
Bray .... **11** E2
Bray-sur-Seine .... **19** D2
Brécey .... **16** B2
Brecht .... **5** D2
Breda .... **5** D3
Bredene .... **4** A2
Bree .... **5** E1
Bréhal .... **16** B3
Breil-sur-Roya .... **39** F3
Breskens .... **4** B2
Bressuire .... **23** E2
Brest .... **14** A2
Bretenoux .... **36** B3
Breteuil .... **17** E2
Breteuil-sur-Noye .... **11** D1
Brezolles .... **17** F2
Briançon .... **33** D1
Briare .... **25** E3
Bricquebec .... **16** B4
Briec .... **14** B2
Brie-Comte-Robert .... **18** C3
Brielle .... **4** C3
Brienne-le-Château .... **19** F2
Briey .... **13** E2
Brignogan .... **14** A3
Brignoles .... **39** D2
Brignoud .... **32** C2
Brionne .... **17** E3
Brioude .... **37** D4
Brioux .... **29** D3
Briouze .... **16** C2
Brissac-Quincé .... **23** E3
Brive-la-Gaillarde .... **36** A3
Broglie .... **17** E3
Broons .... **15** E2
Brossac .... **35** D4
Brou .... **17** F1
Brouvelieures .... **21** D2
Brouwershaven .... **4** C3
Brugge .... **4** B2
Brûlon .... **23** F4
Brumath .... **21** E3
Brummen .... **6** B3
Bruniquel .... **36** A1
Brunssum .... **5** F1
Brussel (Bruxelles) .... **4** C1
Bruxelles (Brussel) .... **4** C1
Bruyères .... **21** D2
Bubry .... **14** C1
Buchy .... **10** C1

Bourbonne-les-Bains .... **20** B2
Bourbourg .... **11** D4
Bourbriac .... **14** C2
Bourdeaux .... **38** B4
Bourg .... **34** C3
Bourg-Achard .... **17** E3
Bourganeuf .... **30** B2
Bourg-Argental .... **37** F4
Bourg-de-Péage .... **32** B2
Bourg-en-Bresse .... **32** B4
Bourges .... **25** D2
Bourg-Lastic .... **30** C2
Bourg-Madame .... **42** B1
Bourgneuf-en-Retz .... **22** C2
Bourgogne .... **12** B2
Bourgoin-Jallieu .... **32** B3
Bourg-St-Andéol .... **38** A4
Bourg-St-Maurice .... **33** E3

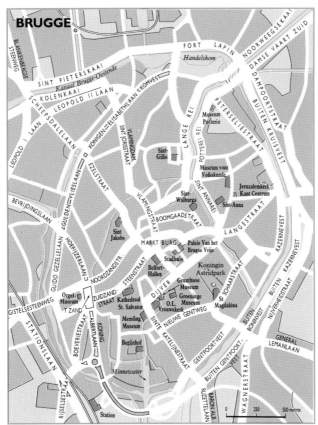

Bucquoy .... 11 ...... E2
Bugeat .... 30 ...... B1
Buis-les-Baronnies .... 38 ...... B3
Buitenpost .... 3 ...... D3
Bulgnéville .... 20 ...... C2
Burgh-Haamstede .... 4 ...... B3
Burie .... 28 ...... C2
Bussang .... 21 ...... D1
Bussum .... 5 ...... E4
Bütgenbach .... 9 ...... E3
Buxy .... 26 ...... B2
Buzançais .... 24 ...... C2
Buzancy .... 13 ...... D2

Calais .... 11 ...... D4
Calenzana .... 44 ...... B3
Calignac .... 35 ...... E1
Callac .... 14 ...... C2
Calvi .... 44 ...... B3
Camarès .... 42 ...... C4
Camaret .... 14 ...... A2
Cambo-les-Bains .... 40 ...... A3
Cambrai .... 12 ...... A4
Cambremer .... 17 ...... D3
Campan .... 41 ...... D2
Cancale .... 15 ...... E3
Cancon .... 35 ...... E2
Candé .... 23 ...... D3
Canet-Plage .... 43 ...... D1
Cannes .... 39 ...... E2
Cany-Barville .... 10 ...... B2
Capbreton .... 40 ...... A3
Cap-d'Ail .... 39 ...... F2
Capendu .... 42 ...... C2
Capestang .... 43 ...... D2
Cap Ferret .... 34 ...... B3
Cap Gris Nez .... 11 ...... D4
Captieux .... 34 ...... C2
Caraman .... 42 ...... A3
Carantec .... 14 ...... B3
Carbon-Blanc .... 34 ...... C3
Carbonne .... 41 ...... F2

C

Cabourg .... 17 ...... D3
Cabrerets .... 36 ...... A2
Cadenet .... 38 ...... B2
Cadillac .... 34 ...... C2
Caen .... 16 ...... C3
Cagnes .... 39 ...... E2
Cahors .... 36 ...... A2
Cajarc .... 36 ...... B2
Calacuccia .... 44 ...... B3

Carcans	**34**	B3	Chalamont	**32**	B4
Carcans Plage	**34**	B3	Chalampé	**21**	E1
Carcassonne	**42**	B2	Challans	**22**	C2
Carcès	**39**	D2	Challes-les-Eaux	**32**	C3
Carennac	**36**	A3	Chalonnes	**23**	E3
Carenton	**16**	B3	Châlons-sur-Marne	**19**	E3
Cargése	**44**	A2	Chalon-sur-Saône	**26**	C2
Carhaix-Plouguer	**14**	C2	Châlus	**29**	F2
Carignan	**13**	D3	Chambéry	**32**	C3
Carling	**13**	F2	Chambley	**13**	E2
Carmaux	**36**	B1	Chambon-sur-Lac	**30**	C1
Carnac	**22**	A3	Chambon-sur-Voueize	**30**	C3
Carpentras	**38**	B3	Chambord	**24**	C3
Carquefou	**23**	D3	Chamonix	**33**	E4
Carqueiranne	**39**	D1	Champagne-Mouton	**29**	E2
Carro	**38**	B1	Champagnole	**27**	D2
Carrouges	**17**	D2	Champaubert	**19**	D3
Carry-le-Rouet	**38**	B1	Champdeniers	**28**	C3
Carteret	**16**	A4	Champeix	**31**	D1
Carvin	**11**	E3	Champier	**32**	B2
Casamozza	**44**	C3	Champigné	**23**	E3
Cassagnes-Bégonhès	**36**	C1	Champillon	**12**	B2
Cassel	**11**	E4	Champlitte	**27**	D4
Cassis	**38**	C1	Champlon	**9**	D3
Casteau	**8**	B4	Champtoceaux	**23**	D3
Casteljaloux	**35**	D2	Chanas	**32**	A2
Castellane	**39**	D3	Chantelle	**31**	D3
Castelmoron	**35**	E2	Chantemerle	**33**	D1
Castelnaudary	**42**	B2	Chantilly	**18**	B4
Castelnau-de-Médoc	**34**	C3	Chantonnay	**23**	D1
Castelnau-de-Montmiral	**42**	B4	Chaource	**19**	E1
Castelnau-Magnoac	**41**	E2	Chapelle-Royale	**17**	E1
Castelsarrasin	**41**	F4	Charavines	**32**	C2
Castets	**40**	B4	Charenton-sur-Cher	**25**	E2
Castillon-la-Bataille	**35**	D3	Charleroi	**8**	B3
Castillonnès	**35**	E2	Charleville-Mézières	**12**	C3
Castres	**42**	B3	Charlieu	**31**	E3
Castricum	**2**	B1	Charly	**19**	D3
Castries	**43**	E3	Charmes	**20**	C2
Catus	**35**	F2	Charny	**25**	E4
Caudebec	**17**	E4	Charolles	**31**	E3
Caudry	**12**	A4	Chârost	**25**	D2
Caumont	**16**	C3	Charroux	**29**	E3
Caunes	**42**	C2	Chartres	**18**	A2
Cauro	**44**	B2	Chassigny	**20**	B1
Caussade	**36**	A1	Château-Arnoux	**38**	C3
Cauterets	**41**	D1	Châteaubourg	**16**	B1
Cauville	**10**	A1	Châteaubriant	**23**	D3
Cavaillon	**38**	B2	Château-Chinon	**26**	A3
Cavalaire-sur-Mer	**39**	D1	Château-du-Loir	**24**	A4
Cavalière	**39**	D1	Châteaudun	**17**	F1
Caylus	**36**	A2	Châteaugiron	**23**	D4
Cazals	**35**	F2	Château-Gontier	**23**	E4
Cazères	**41**	F2	Château-la-Vallière	**24**	A3
Centuri	**44**	C4	Châteaulin	**14**	B2
Cerbere	**43**	D1	Châteaumeillant	**30**	B3
Céret	**42**	C1	Châteauneuf	**29**	D2
Cérilly	**30**	C4	Châteauneuf-de-Faou	**14**	B2
Cerisiers	**19**	D2	Châteauneuf-de-Randon	**37**	E2
Cerizay	**23**	E2	Châteauneuf-du-Pape	**38**	B3
Cernay	**21**	E1	Châteauneuf-en-Thymerais	**17**	F2
Cervione	**44**	C3	Châteauneuf-sur-Cher	**25**	D2
Ceyzériat	**32**	B4	Châteauneuf-sur-Loire	**25**	D4
Chabanais	**29**	E2	Châteauneuf-sur-Sarthe	**23**	E3
Chabeuil	**32**	B1	Châteauponsac	**29**	F3
Chablis	**26**	A4	Château-Porcien	**12**	C3
Chabreloch	**31**	E2	Château-Queyras	**33**	E1
Chabris	**24**	C3	Châteaurenard	**18**	C1
Chagny	**26**	B2	Château-Renault	**24**	B3
Chaillé-les-Marais	**28**	B3	Châteauroux	**24**	C2
Chalabre	**42**	B2	Château-Salins	**21**	D3
Chalais	**35**	D4	Château-Thierry	**19**	D3

Chateauvillain

Châteauvillain	20	A2
Chatel	27	F1
Châtelaillon-Plage	28	B3
Châtelet	8	B3
Châtelguyon	31	D2
Châtellerault	24	A2
Châtelus-Malvaleix	30	B3
Châtenois	20	C2
Châtillon-Coligny	25	E4
Châtillon-en-Bazois	25	F2
Châtillon-en-Diois	32	C1
Châtillon-sur-Chalaronne	32	B4
Châtillon-sur-Indre	24	B2
Châtillon-sur-Loire	25	E3
Châtillon-sur-Marne	12	B2
Châtillon-sur-Seine	19	F1
Chaudes-Aigues	37	D3
Chauffailles	31	F3
Chaufour	18	A3
Chaumergy	27	D2
Chaumont	20	B2
Chaumont	24	B3
Chaunay	29	D3
Chauny	12	A3
Chaussin	26	C3
Chauvigny	29	E4
Chazelles	31	F2
Chef-Boutonne	29	D3
Chemillé	23	E2
Chemin	26	C3
Chénérailles	30	B3
Chenonceaux	24	B3
Cherbourg	16	B4
Chéroy	18	C2
Chevagnes	31	D4
Chevanceaux	35	D4
Chevreuse	18	B3
Chimay	8	B3
Chinon	24	A3
Cholêt	23	E2
Chorges	39	D4
Choye	27	D3
Ciboure	40	A3
Cierp	41	E2
Ciney	8	C3
Cintegabelle	42	A2
Cirey	21	D3
Civray	29	D3
Civrieux-d'A.	32	A3
Clairvaux-les-Lacs	27	D2
Clamecy	25	F3
Clavière	33	E1
Clécy	16	C3
Clefmont	20	B2
Clelles	32	C1
Clères	10	C1
Clermont	18	B4
Clermont-en-Argonne	13	D2
Clermont-Ferrand	31	D2
Clermont-l'Hérault	43	D3
Clerval	27	E3
Clervaux	9	E2
Cléry	24	C4
Clisson	23	D2
Cloyes	24	B4
Cluny	26	B2
Cluses	33	D4
Coevorden	3	E2
Cognac	28	C2
Cogolin	39	D1
Coligny	26	C1
Collinée	15	D2

Collioure	43	D1
Collonges	32	C4
Colmar	21	E2
Colmars	39	D3
Cologne	41	E3
Colombey-les-Belles	20	C3
Colombey-les-deux-Eglises	20	A2
Combeaufontaine	20	C1
Combourg	15	E2
Combronde	31	D2

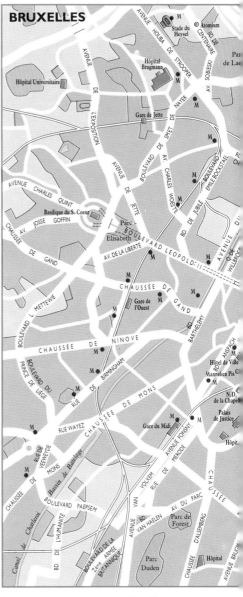

Commentry

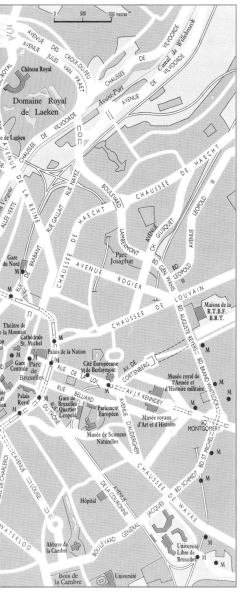

Condrieu	**32**	A2
Conflans	**13**	E2
Confolens	**29**	E2
Conlie	**17**	D1
Connerré	**17**	E1
Conques	**36**	C2
Contay	**11**	E2
Contres	**24**	C3
Contrexéville	**20**	C2
Conty	**11**	D1
Coray	**14**	B1
Corbeil-Essonnes	**18**	B2
Corbie	**11**	E2
Corbigny	**26**	A3
Corcieux	**21**	D2
Cordes	**36**	B1
Corlay	**14**	C2
Cormainville	**18**	A2
Cormeilles	**17**	E3
Cormery	**24**	B3
Cornimont	**21**	D2
Corps	**32**	C1
Corte	**44**	B3
Cosne	**25**	E3
Cosne d'Allier	**30**	C3
Cossé-le-Vivien	**23**	E4
Cotignac	**39**	D2
Couches	**26**	B2
Coucy	**12**	A2
Couhé	**29**	D3
Couilly	**18**	C3
Couiza	**42**	B2
Coulommiers	**18**	C3
Coulon	**28**	C3
Coulonges	**28**	C3
Couptrain	**16**	C2
Courcheval	**33**	D2
Cour-Cheverny	**24**	C3
Courçon	**28**	C3
Courpière	**31**	D2
Courseulles-sur-Mer	**16**	C3
Courson-les-Carrières	**25**	F4
Courteilles	**17**	E3
Courtenay	**18**	C1
Courtomer	**17**	D2
Courtrai (Kortrijk)	**4**	B1
Courville	**17**	F2
Coutainville	**16**	B3
Coutances	**16**	B3
Couterne	**16**	C2
Coutevroult	**18**	C3
Coutras	**35**	D3
Couvin	**8**	B3
Cozes	**28**	C2
Craon	**23**	E4
Craponne-sur-Arzon	**37**	E4
Creches-sur-Saône	**32**	A4
Crécy	**18**	C3
Crécy-en-Ponthieu	**11**	D3
Crécy-sur-Serre	**12**	B3
Creil	**18**	B4
Crémieu	**32**	B3
Créon	**34**	C3
Crépy-en-Valois	**18**	C4
Crespin	**12**	B4
Cressensac	**36**	A3
Crest	**32**	B1
Creutzwald	**13**	F2
Crèvecœur	**11**	D1
Crocq	**30**	B2
Crozon	**14**	A2
Cruseilles	**32**	C4

Commentry	**30**	C3
Commercy	**20**	B3
Compiègne	**18**	C4
Comps-sur-Artuby	**39**	D2
Concarneau	**14**	B1
Conches	**17**	E3
Condat	**36**	C4
Condé-en-Brie	**19**	D3
Condé-sur-Noireau	**16**	C2
Condom	**41**	D4

Cruzy	42	C3
Cuers	39	D1
Cuijk	5	F3
Cuiseaux	26	C2
Cuisery	26	C2
Culan	30	B3
Culemborg	5	E3
Culoz	32	C3
Cusset	31	D3
Cuvilly	11	E1

D

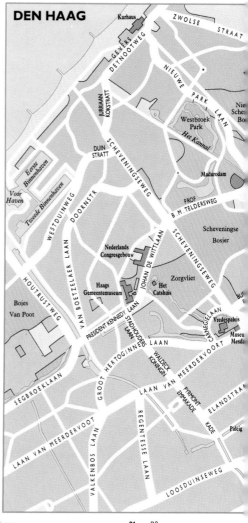

DEN HAAG

Dabo	21	E3
Dammartin-en-Goële	18	C3
Dampierre	27	D3
Dampierre-sur-Boutonne	28	C3
Dampierre-sur-Salon	27	D4
Damville	17	F2
Damvillers	13	D2
Dangé-St-Romain	24	A2
Dannemarie	21	E1
Daoulas	14	A2
Darney	20	C2
Dax	40	B3
Deauville	17	D3
Decazeville	36	B2
Decize	25	F2
De Cocksdorp	2	C3
Dedemsvaart	3	E1
De Haan	4	A2
Deinze	4	B1
De Koog	2	C3
De Kooy	2	C2
Delden	6	B4
Delft	4	C3
Delfzijl	3	F3
Delle	21	D1
Delme	20	C4
Denain	12	A4
Den Burg	2	C2
Dendermonde	4	C1
Denekamp	6	C4
Den Haag	4	C4
Den Helder	2	B2
Den Oever	2	C2
De Panne	4	A2
Derval	22	C3
Descartes	24	B2
Desvres	11	D3
Deurne	5	E2
Deventer	6	B4
Die	32	B1
Diekirch	9	E2
Dieppe	10	C2
Dieren	6	B3
Diest	5	D1
Dieulefit	38	B4
Dieulourard	20	C3
Dieuze	21	D3
Diever	3	E2
Differdange	9	D1
Digne	39	D3
Digoin	31	E3
Dijon	26	C3
Diksmuide	4	A2
Dinan	15	E2
Dinant	8	C3
Dinard	15	E3
Dinoze	21	D2
Dissel	17	F3
Dives-sur-Mer	17	D3
Divonne	27	E1
Doesburg	6	B3
Doetinchem	6	B3
Dokkum	3	D3
Dol-de-Bretagne	15	E2
Dole	27	D3
Dombasle	20	C3
Dombrot-le-Sec	20	C2
Domburg	4	B3
Domèvre-en-Haye	20	C3
Domfront	16	C2
Domme	35	F3
Dompaire	20	C2
Dompierre	31	E3
Domrémy-la-Pucelle	20	B3

(Map of Den Haag / The Hague area with labels: Van Alkemadelaan, Landscheidingsweg, Klein Zwitserland, Oude Waalsdorperweg, Hubertus Park, Vaalsdorperweg, St Annalands, Chingendael, Plesmanweg, Hubertus Viaduct, Oostduin Arendsdorp, Raamweg, Wassenaarseweg, Weg, Laan Copes Van Cattenburch, Stadhuis, Java Straat, Benoordenhoutseweg, Koningskade, Haagse Bos, Laan Van Nieuw Oost Indië, Zuidenhoutseweg, Alexanderstraat, Mauritskade, Parkstraat, Hogewal, Musée Meermanno-Westreenianum, Klooster Kerk, Paleis, Kostuum Museum, Koecamp, Juliana Van Stolberglaan, Haags Historisch Museum, Mauritshuis, Noordeinde, Centraal Station, Ouid Raadhuis, Hofweg, Binnenhof, Kalver Markt, Grote Kerk, Grote Markt Straat, Theater, Prinsegracht, Spui, Prins Bernhard Viaduct, Utrechtse Baan, Zieken, Station HS)

Doulevant-le-Château	20	A2
Doullens	11	E2
Dourdan	18	B2
Douvaine	27	E1
Douzy	13	D3
Dozulé	17	D3
Drachten	3	D2
Draguignan	39	D2
Dreux	17	D2
Driebergen	5	E3
Dronten	3	D1
Drusenheim	21	F3
Druten	5	E3
Ducey	16	B2
Duclair	17	E4
Dudelange	9	E1
Duingt	33	D3
Dun	13	D2
Dunkerque	11	E4
Dunkerque Ouest	11	D4
Dun-le-Palestel	30	A3
Dun-sur-Auron	25	E2
Duras	35	D3
Durban-Corbières	42	C2
Durbury	9	D3
Durtal	23	F3
Dwingeloo	3	E2

E

Eaux-Bonnes	40	C2
Eaux-Chaudes	40	C2
Eauze	41	D4
Ebreuil	31	D3
Echallon	32	C4
Echternach	9	E2
Ecommoy	24	A4
Ecouis	18	A4
Ecueillé	24	C2
Ecury	19	E3
Edam	2	C1
Ede	5	E3
Eeklo	4	B2
Eelde-Paterswolde	3	E3
Eghezée	8	C4
Egletons	30	B1
Egmond aan Zee	2	B2
Eguzon	30	A3
Ehnen	9	E1
Eibergen	6	B3
Eindhoven	5	E2
Elbeuf	17	E3
Elburg	3	D1
Elne	42	C1
Elst	5	F3
Embrun	39	D4
Emmeloord	3	D2
Emmen	3	E2
Enghien	8	B4
Englefontaine	12	B4
Enkhuizen	2	C2
Enschede	6	C4
Ensisheim	21	E1
Entraygues-sur-Truyère	36	C2
Entrevaux	39	E3
Epannes	28	C3
Epe	6	A4
Épernay	19	E3
Epernon	18	A3

Dontilly	18	C2
Donzenac	36	A4
Donzère	38	A4
Donzy	25	E3
Doorn	5	E3
Doornik (Tournai)	8	A4
Dordives	18	C2
Dordrecht	5	D3
Dormans	12	B2
Dornes	25	F2
Dortan	27	D1
Douai	11	F3
Douarnenez	14	A2
Douchy	18	C1
Doucier	27	D2
Doudeville	10	B1
Doué-la-Fontaine	23	F2
Doulaincourt	20	B2

Épinal	21	D2
Epône	18	A3
Erbalunga	44	C4
Ermelo	5	E4
Ermenonville	18	C4
Erneé	16	B1
Erquy	15	D3
Erstein	21	E3
Ervy-le-Châtel	19	E1
Esch	9	D2
Esch-sur-Alzette	9	D1
Espalion	36	C2
Espelette	40	A3
Estagel	42	C1
Estaires	11	E3
Esternay	19	D3
Estissac	19	E2
Estrées-St-Denis	18	C4
Étables-sur-Mer	15	D3
Etain	13	E2
Etalle	9	D2
Étampes	18	B2
Etaples	11	D3
Etretat	10	A1
Ettelbruck	9	E2
Eu	10	C2
Eupen	9	E4
Europoort	4	C3
Evaux-les-Bains	30	C3
Evian	27	E1
Evisa	44	B3
Evran	15	E2
Evreux	17	F3
Evron	16	C1
Evry	18	B3
Excideuil	35	F4
Exmes	17	D2
Eygvieres	38	B2
Eygurande	30	C2
Eymet	35	E3
Eymoutiers	30	A2

F

Facture	34	B3
Falaise	17	D3
Fanjeaux	42	B2
Farebersviller	21	D4
Faucogney	21	D1
Faulquemont	13	F2
Fauville	10	B1
Faverges	33	D3
Faverney	20	C1
Fayence	39	E2
Fayl-Billot	20	B1
Fécamp	10	B2
Felletin	30	B2
Fénétrange	21	D4
Fère-Champenoise	19	E3
Fère-en-Tardenois	12	A2
Ferrette	21	E1
Ferrières	18	C1
Feurs	31	E2
Figari	44	B1
Figeac	36	B2
Firminy	37	E4
Fismes	12	B2
Flaine	33	D4
Flavigny-sur-Moselle	20	C3

Flers	16	C2
Fleurance	41	E3
Fleuré	29	E3
Fleurus	8	B3
Fleury	17	F3
Flins	18	B3
Flize	12	C3
Flogny-la-Chapelle	19	E1
Florac	37	D2
Florennes	8	B3
Florenville	8	C2
Flumet	33	D3
Foix	42	A2
Fontainebleau	18	C2
Fontaine-Française	26	C4
Fontaine-le-Dun	10	B2
Fontenay-le-Comte	28	C3
Fontenay-Trésigny	18	C3
Font-Romeu	42	B1
Forbach	21	D4
Forcalquier	38	C3
Forges-les-Eaux	10	C1
Formerie	11	D1
Fos	41	E1
Fosses	8	C3
Fos-sur-Mer	38	B2
Foucarmont	10	C2
Fouesnant	14	B1
Fougères	16	B1
Fougerolles	21	D1
Foulain	20	B2
Fouras	28	B2
Fourcès	41	D4
Fourmies	12	B4
Fournels	37	D3
Fours	26	A2
Fraize	21	D2
Francardo	44	B3
Franeker	3	D3
Frangy	32	C4
Frayssinet	36	A2
Fréjus	39	E2
Fresnay-sur-Sarthe	17	D1
Fresnes	11	E3
Fresnes	20	C2
Fresnes-en-Woëvre	13	E2
Fréteval	24	B4
Fretigney	27	D4
Frévent	11	E3
Freyming Merlebach	13	F2
Froissy	11	D1
Fromentel	16	C2
Fronsac	41	E2
Frontignan	43	E3
Fruges	11	D3
Fumay	12	C3
Fumel	35	E2
Furnès (Veurne)	4	A2

G

Gabarret	41	D4
Gacé	17	D2
Gaël	15	E1
Gaillac	42	B4
Gaillon	17	F3
Gallargues	43	E3
Gamaches	10	C2
Gan	40	C2

Gand (Gent) .... **4** B1
Ganges .... **43** E4
Gannat .... **31** D3
Gap .... **39** D4
Gardanne .... **38** C2
Gavarnie .... **41** D1
Gavray .... **16** B3
Gedinne .... **8** C2
Geel .... **5** D2
Geertruidenberg .... **5** D3
Geldrop .... **5** E2
Geleen .... **5** E1
Gembloux .... **8** C4
Gémenos .... **38** C1
Gemert .... **5** E2
Gémozac .... **28** C2
Genappe .... **8** B4
Gençay .... **29** E3
Génelard .... **26** B2
Genk .... **5** E1
Genlis .... **26** C3
Gennes .... **23** F3
Gennep .... **5** F3
Génolhac .... **37** E2
Gent (Gand) .... **4** B1
Gentioux .... **30** B2
Geraardsbergen .... **4** C1
Gérardmer .... **21** D2
Gerbéviller .... **21** D3
Germay .... **20** B3
Gevrey-Chambertin .... **26** C3
Gex .... **27** E1
Ghisonaccia .... **44** C2
Ghisoni .... **44** B2
Gien .... **25** E4
Giens .... **39** D1
Gieten .... **3** E2
Giethoorn .... **3** D2
Gignac .... **43** D3
Gimont .... **41** E3
Giromagny .... **21** D1
Gisors .... **18** A4
Gistel .... **4** A2
Givet .... **12** C4
Givors .... **32** A3
Givry .... **26** B2
Givry .... **8** B3
Givry-en-Argonne .... **20** A4
Gizeux .... **24** A3
Glénic .... **30** B3
Goderville .... **10** B1
Goes .... **4** C2
Goirle .... **5** D2
Golfe Juan .... **39** E2
Goncelin .... **32** C2
Gondrecourt .... **20** B3
Gondrin .... **41** D4
Goor .... **6** B4
Gordes .... **38** B3
Gorinchem .... **5** D3
Gorredijk .... **3** D2
Gorron .... **16** C2
Gosselies .... **8** B3
Gouarec .... **14** C2
Gouda .... **5** D3
Goumois .... **27** F3
Gourdon .... **36** A3
Gourin .... **14** B2
Gournay-en-Bray .... **11** D1
Gouzon .... **30** B3
Graçay .... **24** C2
Gramat .... **36** A3

Grancey .... **26** C4
Grandcamp .... **16** B4
Grand-Champ .... **22** B4
Grande Fougeray .... **22** C4
Grandpré .... **12** C2
Grandrieu .... **37** E3
Grandvilliers .... **11** D1
Granges-sur-Vologne .... **21** D2
Granville .... **16** B3
Grasse .... **39** E2
Graulhet .... **42** B3
Grave .... **5** E3
Gravelines .... **11** D4
Gray .... **27** D4
Grenade .... **40** C3
Grenade .... **41** F3
Grenoble .... **32** C2
Gréoux-les-Bains .... **38** C2
Grevenmacher .... **9** E2
Grez-en-Bouère .... **23** E4
Grignan .... **38** B4
Grignols .... **35** D2
Grimaud .... **39** D1
Grisolles .... **41** F3
Groenlo .... **6** B3
Groningen .... **3** E3
Grostenquin .... **13** F1
Grouw .... **3** D2
Gruissan .... **43** D2
Guebwiller .... **21** E2
Guémené-Penfao .... **22** C3
Guer .... **22** C4
Guérande .... **22** B3
Guéret .... **30** B3
Guérigny .... **25** F2
Guethary .... **40** A3
Gueugnon .... **26** A2
Guichen .... **22** C4
Guignes .... **18** C3
Guillaumes .... **39** E3
Guillestre .... **33** D1
Guilvinec .... **14** A1
Guînes .... **11** D4
Guingamp .... **14** C2
Guipry .... **22** C4
Guise .... **12** B3
Guîtres .... **35** D3
Gujan-Mestras .... **34** B3
Gy .... **27** D3

H

Haaksbergen .... **6** C4
Haarlem .... **2** B1
Habay .... **9** D2
Hagetmau .... **40** C3
Hagondange .... **13** E2
Haguenau .... **21** F4
Halle .... **8** B4
Halsteren .... **4** C2
Ham .... **11** F1
Hamoir .... **9** D3
Hannut .... **8** C4
Hans-sur-Lesse .... **8** C3
Hardelot-Plage .... **10** C3
Hardenberg .... **3** E1
Harderwijk .... **5** E4
Haren .... **3** E3
Harfleur .... **17** D4

Harlingen

Harlingen	2	C3	
Haroué	20	C3	
Hasparren	40	B3	
Hasselt	3	D1	
Hasselt	5	D1	
Hattem	3	D1	
Haut-Asco	44	B3	
Hauteville Plage	16	B3	
Havelange	8	C3	
Hayange	13	E2	
Hazebrouck	11	E4	
Hechtel	5	E1	
Hédé	15	E2	
Heemsted	2	B1	
Heerde	3	D1	
Heerenveen	3	D2	
Heerlen	5	F1	
Heeze	5	E2	
Heino	3	D1	
Heist	4	B2	
Hellendoorn	3	E1	
Hellevoetsluis	4	C3	
Helmond	5	E2	
Hëming	21	D3	
Hendaye	40	A3	
Hengelo	6	C4	
Hénin Beaumont	11	E3	
Hennebont	22	A4	
Henrichement	25	D3	
Herbault	24	B3	
Herbestnal	9	E4	
Herbeumont	8	C2	
Herentals	5	D2	
Héricourt	27	E4	
Hérisson	30	C3	
Herment	30	C2	
Herselt	5	D1	
Hesdin	11	D3	
Hettange	13	E2	
Heyrieux	32	B3	
Hiersac	29	D2	
Hillegom	5	D4	
Hilvarenbeek	5	E2	
Hilversum	5	E4	
Hirsingue	21	E1	
Hirson	12	B3	
Hochfelden	21	E3	
Hoedekenskerre	4	C2	
Hoek van Holland	4	C3	
Hollum	3	D3	
Holten	6	B4	
Holwerd	3	D3	
Homps	42	C2	
Honfleur	17	D4	
Hoogerheide	4	C2	
Hoogeveen	3	E2	
Hoogezand	3	E3	
Hoogkarspel	2	C2	
Hoogstraten	5	D2	
Hoorn	2	C2	
Hordain	12	A4	
Hornoy	11	D2	
Horst	5	F2	
Hossegor	40	A3	
Hostens	34	C2	
Hotton	9	D3	
Houdain	11	E3	
Houdan	18	A3	
Houdelaincourt	20	B3	
Houeillès	35	D2	
Houffalize	9	D3	
Houlgate	17	D3	
Hourtin	33	B4	
Hourtin Plage	34	B4	
Hucqueliers	11	D3	
Huelgoat	14	B2	
Huizen	2	C2	
Hulst	4	C2	
Huriel	30	C3	
Huy	8	C3	
Hyeres	39	D1	

I

Ieper (Ypres)	4	A1	
Ijmuiden	2	B1	
Illiers	17	E1	
Imphy	25	F2	
Ingelmunster	4	B1	
Ingwiller	21	E4	
Isdes	25	D4	
Isigny	16	B3	
Isola	39	E3	
Isola 2000	39	E3	
Issoire	31	D1	
Issoudun	25	D2	
Is-sur-Tille	26	C4	
Istres	38	B2	
Itxassou	40	A3	
Ivry-la-Bataille	18	A3	
Izegem	4	B1	
Izenore	32	C4	

J

Jaligny-sur-Besbre	31	D3	
Janville	18	B2	
Janzé	23	D4	
Jard-sur-Mer	28	B3	
Jargeau	25	D4	
Jarnac	29	D2	
Jarnages	30	B3	
Jarny	13	E2	
Jausiers	39	E4	
Javron	16	C2	
Jeumont	12	B4	
Jodoigne	8	C4	
Joigny	19	D1	
Joinville	20	B3	
Jonzac	28	C1	
Josselin	15	D1	
Jougne	27	E2	
Joure	3	D2	
Joyeuse	37	E2	
Juan-les-Pins	39	E2	
Jugon	15	E2	
Juillac	35	F4	
Jullouville	16	B2	
Jumeaux	31	D1	
Jumièges	17	E4	
Juniville	12	C2	
Jussey	20	C1	
Juvigny-le-Tertre	16	B2	
Juzennecourt	20	A2	

K

Kaatsheuvel	5	D3
Kampen	3	D1
Kasterlee	5	D2
Katwijk aan Zee	4	C4
Kaysersberg	21	E2
Kerkrade	5	F1
Klazienaveen	3	F2
Knokke-Heist	4	B2
Koksijde-Bad	4	A2
Kortrijk (Courtrai)	4	B1
Kotten	6	B3
Krimpen	5	D3
Kruiningen	4	C2

L

La Bassée	11	E3
Labastide-d'Armagnac	41	D4
Labastide-Murat	36	A2
La Bastide-Puylaurent	37	E2
La Bastode de-Sérou	42	A2
La Bâtie-Neuve	39	D4
La Baule	22	B3
La Bazouche-Gouët	17	E1
La Belle Etoile	19	E2
Labenne	40	A3
La Bérarde	33	D1
L'Aber-Wrac'h	14	A3
Labouheyre	34	B2
La Bourboule	30	C1
Labréde	34	C3
La Bresse	21	D2
La Brillane	38	C3
Labrit	34	C1
Lacanau	34	B3
Lacanau-Océan	34	B3
La Canourgue	37	D2
La Capelle	12	B3
Lacapelle-Marival	36	B3
La Capte	39	D1
La Cateau	12	A4
Lacaune	42	C3
La Cavalerie	37	D1
La Celle-Dunoise	30	B3
La Chaise Dieu	37	E4
La Chambre	33	D2
La Chapelle	32	A4
La Chapelle-d'Angillon	25	D3
La Chapelle-en-Vercors	32	B1
La Chapelle-Glain	23	D3
La Charité	25	E2
La Chartre	24	A4
La Châtaigneraie	28	C4
La Châtre	30	B4
La Ciotat	38	C1
La Clayette	31	F3
La Clusaz	33	D3
La Cluse	32	C4
La Cluse-et-Mijoux	27	E2
La Coquille	29	F1
La Côte-St-Andre	32	B2
La Courtine	30	B2
Lacq	40	C3
La Croisère	30	A3
La Croixille	16	B1
La Croix-Valmer	39	E1
La Cure	27	E1
Ladon	18	C1
La Fère	12	A3
Laferté	20	B1
La Ferté-Bernard	17	E1
La Ferté Gaucher	19	D3
La Ferté Macé	16	C2
La Ferté-Milon	18	C4
La Ferté-sous-Jouarre	18	C3
La Ferté-St-Aubin	25	D4
La Ferté-Vidame	17	E2
Laffrey	32	C2
La Flèche	23	F3
La Flotte	28	B3
Lafrançaise	35	F1
La Gacilly	22	C4
La Garde-Freinet	39	D1
Lagniueu	32	B3
Lagny	18	C3
La Grand-Combe	37	E1
La Grande-Motte	43	E3
Lagrasse	42	C2
La Grave	33	D2
Laguepie	36	B1
La Guerche	25	E2
La Guerche-de-Bretagne	23	D4
Laguiole	36	C2
La Haye-du-Puits	16	B3
La Hutte	17	D1
L'Aigle	17	E2
Laignes	19	E1
L'Aiguillon	28	B3
Laissac	36	C2
La Javie	39	D3
Lalinde	35	E3
La Loupe	17	E2
Lalouvesc	37	F3
La Louvière	8	B3
L'Alpe-d'Huez	32	C2
La Machine	25	F2
La Malène	37	D2
Lamalou-les-Bains	43	D3
Lamarche	20	C2
Lamarque	34	C3
Lamastre	32	A1
La Maucarrière	23	F1
Lamballe	15	D2
Lambesc	38	B2
La Mongie	41	D2
La Mothe-Achard	28	A4
Lamotte-Beuvron	25	D3
La Motte-Chalancon	38	B4
Lampaul-Plourzel	14	A2
La Mure	32	C1
Lamure	31	F2
La Napoule-Plage	39	E2
Landerneau	14	B2
Landévennec	14	A2
Landivisiau	14	B2
Landivy	16	B2
Landrecies	12	B4
La Neuve-Lyre	17	E3
Langeac	37	D3
Langeais	24	A3
Langentière	37	F2
Langogne	37	E3
Langoiran	34	C3
Langon	35	D2
Langres	20	B1

Lanmeur	14	B3
Lannemezan	41	D2
Lannilis	14	A3
Lannion	14	C3
Lanouaille	29	F1
Lanslebourg	33	E2
Lantosque	39	F3
Lanvollon	14	C3
Laon	12	B3
La Pacaudière	31	E3
Lapalisse	31	D3
La Pallice	28	B3
La Palmyre	28	B2
La Palud-sur-Verdon	39	D2
La Petite-Pierre	21	E4
La Plagne	33	D3
Laplume	35	E1
Lapoutroie	21	E2
Laragne-Montéglin	38	C3
L'Arbresle	32	A3
Larche	36	A3
Larche	39	E4
La Réole	35	D2
L'Argentière-la-Bessée	33	D1
Larmor	22	A4
La Roche-Bernard	22	B3
La Roche-Chalais	35	D4
La Roche-en-Ardenne	9	D3
La Rochefoucauld	29	E2
La Rochelle	28	B3
La Roche-Posay	24	B2
La-Roches-sur-Foron	33	D4
La Roche-sur-Yon	23	D1
La Rochette	33	D2
Larochette	9	E2
Laroquebrou	36	B3
La Roquebrussanne	39	D1
Laroque-des-Arcs	36	A2
La Roque-Gageac	35	F3
Larrau	40	B2
Laruns	40	C2
La Salvetat	36	B2
La Salvetat-sur-Agout	42	C3
La Seyne	38	C1
La Souterraine	30	A3
Lassay	16	C2
Lassigny	11	E1
La Suze	23	F4
Latour de Carol	42	B1
La Tour-du-Pin	32	B3
La Tranche-sur-Mer	28	B3
La Tremblade	28	B2
La Trimouille	29	F3
La Trinité	22	A3
La Trinité-Porhoët	15	D1
La Turbie	39	F2
Laubrières	23	D4
Laurière	30	A2
Lauterbourg	21	F4
Lautrec	42	B3
Lauwersoog	3	E3
Lauzerte	35	F2
Lauzun	35	E2
Laval	23	E4
Lavardac	35	D1
Lavaur	42	B3
Lavelanet	42	B2
La Voulte	32	A1
Lavoûte-Chilhac	37	D3
Lavoûte-sur-Loire	37	E3
La Wantezenau	21	F3
Le Bar	39	E2
Le Barp	34	C2
Le Beausset	38	C1
Le Blanc	24	B1
Le Boulou	42	C1
Le Bourg d'Oisans	32	C2
Le Bourget	32	C3
Le Bugue	35	E3
Le Cap d'Agde	43	D2
Le Cateau	12	A4
Le Catelet	12	A3
Le Caylar	43	D4
L'Echalp	33	E1
Le Chateau-d'Oléron	28	B2
Le Châtelard	33	D3
Le Châtelet	30	B4
Le Chesne	12	C2
Le Cheylard	37	F3
Le Conquet	14	A2
Le Creusot	26	B2
Le Croisic	22	B3
Le Crotoy	11	D2
Lectoure	41	E4
Lédignan	43	E4
Le Donjon	31	E3
Le Dorat	29	F3
Leek	3	E3
Leerdam	5	D3
Leeuwarden	3	D3
Le Faou	14	B2
Le Faouët	14	C1
Le Fossat	42	A2
Legé	22	C2
Le Grand Bourg	30	A3
Le Grand-Lucé	24	A4
Le Grand-Pressigny	24	B2
Le Grau-du-Roi	43	E3
Léguevin	41	F3
Le Havre	17	D4
Le Hohwald	21	E3
Leiden	5	D4
Le Lauzet-Ubaye	39	D4
Le Lavandou	39	D1
Le Lion-D'Angers	23	E3
Le Logis-du-Pin	39	E2
Le Loroux Botterau	23	D2
Le Louroux	23	E3
Le Luc	39	D2
Le Lude	24	A4
Lelystad	2	C1
Le Mans	24	A4
Le Markstein	21	D2
Le Mas-d'Azil	41	F2
Le Mayet	31	E3
Lembach	21	E4
Lembeye	41	D3
Le Merlerault	17	D2
Lemmer	3	D2
Le Monastier	37	E3
Le Monêtier	33	D1
Le Mont-Dore	30	C1
Le Montet	31	D3
Le Mont-St Michel	16	B2
Lempdes	31	D2
Le Muret	34	C2
Le Muy	39	E2
Lencloître	24	A2
Le Neubourg	17	E3
Le Nouvion-en-Thierache	12	B4
Lens	11	E3
Léon	40	B4
Leopoldsburg	5	E1
Le Palais	22	A3

Le Péage-de-Rousillon	32	A2
Le Perthus	42	C1
Le Pin-au-Haras	17	D2
Le Pont-de-Beauvoision	32	C3
Le Pont-de-Claix	32	C2
Le Pontet d'Eyrans	34	C4
Le Portel	10	C3
Le Pouldu	22	A4
Le Pouré-sur-Vie	23	D1
Le Pouzin	32	A1
Le Puy	37	E3
Le Quesnoy	12	B4
Le Rabot	25	D4
Le Rozier	37	D1
Le Russey	27	E3
Les Abrets	32	C3
Les Adrets	39	E2
Les Aix	25	E3
Les Andelys	18	A4
Les Arcs	33	E3
Les Arcs	39	D2
Les Baux	38	B2
Les Cabannes	42	A1
Lescar	40	C2
L'Escarène	39	F3
Les Contamines	33	D3
Les Deux-Alpes	33	D2
Les Echarmeaux	31	F3
Les Echelles	32	C2
Les Epesses	23	E2
Les Essarts	23	D1
Les Eyzies	35	F3
Les Gets	33	D4
Les Halles	31	F2
Les Hayons	10	C1
Les Herbiers	23	D2
Les Houches	33	E3
Les Issambres	39	E2
Les Laumes	26	B4
Les Lecques	38	C1
Les Menuires	33	D2
Lesneven	14	A3
Lesparre-Médoc	34	B4
Les Pieux	16	A4
Les Planches	27	D2
Les Ponts-de Ce	23	E3
Les Riceys	19	E1
Les Rosiers	23	F3
Les Rousses	27	E2
Les Sables-d'Olonne	28	A4
Lessay	16	B3
Lessines	8	A4
Lestelle Bétharram	40	C2
Les Trois-Epis	21	E2
Les Trois-Moutiers	23	F2
Les Vans	37	E2
Les Verrières	27	E2
Le Teil	38	A4
Le Teilleul	16	C2
Le Thillot	21	D1
Le Touquet	10	C3
Le Touvet	32	C2
Le Trayas	39	E2
Le Tréport	10	C2
Leucate	43	D2
Leuglay	20	A1
Leuven (Louvain)	5	D1
Leuze	8	A4
Le Val-André	15	D2
Le Vaudreuil	17	F3
Levens	39	F3
Le Vernet	39	D3
Levet	25	D2
Levie	44	B1
Levier	27	E3
Le Vigan	43	D4
Levroux	24	C2
Lezay	29	D3
Lézignan-Corbières	42	C2
Lezoux	31	D2
Libourne	35	D3
Libramont	9	D2
Lichtenvoorde	6	B3
Liege (Luik)	9	D4
Lier	5	D2
Liernais	26	B3
Lieurey	17	E3
Liffré	16	A1
Ligeuville	9	E3
Lignières	25	D2
Ligny-en-Barrois	20	B3
Ligueil	24	B2
L'Ile Rousse	44	B3
Lille	11	F3
Lillebonne	17	E4
Lillers	11	E3
Limoges	29	F2
Limogne	36	A2
Limonest	32	A3
Limours	18	B3
Limoux	42	B2
Lisieux	17	D3
Lisle	42	B4
L'Isle-Adam	18	B4
L'Isle-de-Noé	41	E3
L'Isle-en-Dodon	41	E2
L'Isle-Jourdain	29	E3
L'Isle-Jourdain	41	F3
L'Isle-sur-la-Sorgue	38	B3
L'Isle-sur-le-Doubs	27	E4
Lisse	5	D4
Lit-en-Mixe	34	B1
Livarot	17	D3
Livernon	36	B2
Livron	32	A1
Lizy	18	C3
L'Ile-Bouchard	24	A3
Lochem	6	B4
Loches	24	B2
Locmaria	22	A3
Locmariaquer	22	A3
Locminé	22	B4
Locquirec	14	B3
Locronan	14	B2
Loctudy	14	B1
Lodève	43	D3
Lohéac	22	C4
Lokeren	4	C2
Lombez	41	E3
Lomme	11	F3
Lommel	5	E2
Londinières	10	C2
Longeau	20	B1
Longny	17	E2
Longué	23	F3
Longuyon	13	E2
Longwy	13	E3
Lons-le-Saunier	27	D2
Lorcé	9	D3
Lorentzen	21	E4
Lorgues	39	D2
Lorient	22	A4
Loriol-sur-Drôme	32	A1
Lormes	26	A3

Lormont	34	C3
Lorris	25	D4
Loudéac	15	D2
Loudes	37	E3
Loudun	23	F3
Louhans	26	C2
Loulay	28	C3
Lourdes	41	D2
Louvain (Leuven)	5	D1
Louviers	17	F3
Lubersac	30	A1
Lucenay	26	B3
Luc-en-Diois	38	C4
Luçon	28	B3
Luc-sur-Mer	16	C3
Luigny	17	E1
Luik (Liege)	9	D4
Lumbres	11	D3
Lummen	5	E1
Lunas	43	D5
Lunel	43	E3
Lunéville	21	D3
Lurcy-Lévis	25	E2
Lure	21	D1
Lureuil	24	B2
Luri	44	C4
Lusignan	29	D3
Lusigny	19	E2
Lus-la-Croix-Haute	38	C4
Lussac-les-Châteaux	29	E3
Lussan	37	F1
Luxembourg	9	E1
Luz-St-Sauveur	41	D1
Luzy	26	A2
Lyon	32	A3
Lyons-la-Forêt	18	A4

M

Maaseik	5	E1
Maasmechelen	5	E1
Maassluis	4	C3
Maastricht	5	E1
Machault	12	C2
Machecoul	22	C2
Mâcon	26	C1
Made	5	D3
Magescq	40	B3
Magnac-Laval	29	F3
Magny-en-Vexin	18	A4
Maîche	27	F3
Mailly-le-Camp	19	E3
Maintenon	18	A2
Malaucène	38	B3
Malbuisson	27	E2
Maldegem	4	B2
Malesherbes	18	B2
Malestroit	22	B4
Malicorne	23	F4
Malines (Mechelen)	5	D1
Malmédy	9	E3
Malo-les-Bains	11	E4
Mamers	17	D1
Mandelieu	39	E2
Manosque	38	C2
Mansle	29	D2
Mantes	18	A3
Manzat	30	C2
Marans	28	B3

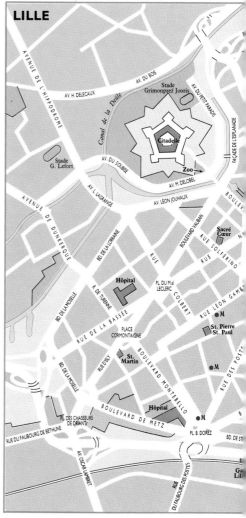

Marboz	26	C1
Marchaux	27	E3
Marche-en-Famenne	9	D3
Marcheprime	34	C3
Marciac	41	D3
Marcigny	31	E3
Marcillac-Vallon	36	C2
Marcillat	30	C3
Marcilly-le-Hayer	19	D2
Marckolsheim	21	E2
Marennes	28	B2
Mareuil	28	B4
Mareuil	29	E1
Marignane	38	B2
Marigny-le-Châtel	19	D2
Marines	18	B4
Maringues	31	D2
Marle	12	B3

Marlenheim

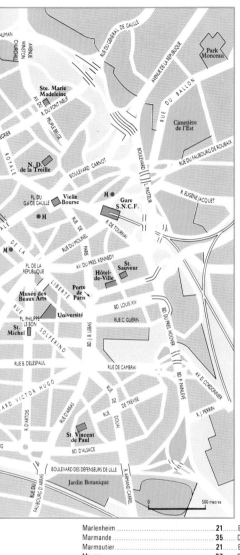

Marlenheim	**21**	E3
Marmande	**35**	D2
Marmoutier	**21**	E3
Marnay	**27**	D3
Marquion	**11**	F2
Marquise	**11**	D4
Marseillan	**43**	D3
Marseillan-Plage	**43**	D2
Marseille	**38**	C1
Marseille-en-Beauvaisis	**11**	D1
Martel	**36**	A3
Martelange	**9**	D2
Martigné-Ferchard	**23**	D4
Martigues	**38**	B2
Marvejols	**37**	D2
Masevaux	**21**	D1
Massat	**41**	F1
Masseube	**41**	E3

Massey	**25**	D2
Massiac	**37**	D4
Matha	**29**	D2
Mathay	**27**	F4
Matignon	**15**	E2
Matour	**31**	F3
Maubeuge	**12**	B4
Maubourguet	**41**	D3
Mauléon	**23**	E2
Mauléon-Licharre	**40**	B2
Maulévrier	**23**	E2
Maupertus	**16**	B4
Maure	**22**	C4
Mauriac	**36**	B4
Mauron	**15**	D1
Maurs	**36**	B3
Maury	**42**	C1
Mauvezin	**41**	E3
Mauze	**28**	C3
Mayenne	**16**	C1
Mayet	**24**	A4
Mazamet	**42**	B3
Mazères	**42**	A2
Meaux	**18**	C3
Mechelen (Malines)	**5**	D1
Medemblik	**2**	C2
Megève	**33**	D3
Mehun	**25**	D2
Meijel	**5**	F2
Mélisey	**21**	D1
Melle	**29**	D3
Melun	**18**	C2
Menan	**4**	A1
Menat	**30**	C3
Mende	**37**	D2
Mens	**32**	C1
Menthon	**33**	D3
Menton	**39**	F2
Meppel	**3**	D2
Mer	**24**	C4
Merdrignac	**15**	D2
Meribel	**33**	D2
Méréville	**18**	B2
Meribal	**33**	D2
Mersch	**9**	E2
Meru	**18**	B4
Mervans	**26**	C2
Méry	**19**	E2
Meschers-sur-Gironde	**28**	B2
Meslay	**23**	E4
Mesnil-Val	**10**	C2
Mesvres	**26**	B2
Metabief	**27**	E2
Méteren	**11**	E4
Mettet	**8**	C3
Metz	**13**	E2
Metzervisse	**13**	F2
Meulan	**18**	B3
Meung	**24**	C4
Meximieux	**32**	B3
Meymac	**30**	B1
Meyrargues	**38**	C2
Meyrueis	**37**	D1
Meyzieu	**32**	B3
Mèze	**43**	E3
Mézel	**39**	D3
Mézières	**29**	E3
Mézièrès-en-Brenne	**24**	B2
Mézilhac	**37**	F3
Mézin	**35**	D1
Middelkerke-Bad	**4**	A2
Middleburg	**4**	B2

Middleharnis	4	C3
Midsland	2	C3
Miélan	41	D3
Migennes	19	D1
Mijoux	27	D1
Millas	42	C1
Millau	37	D1
Milly	18	B2
Mimizan	34	B2
Mimizan-Plage	34	B2
Mindin	22	C3
Miramar	39	E2
Miramas	38	B2
Mirambeau	28	C1
Miramont-de-Guyenne	35	D2
Mirande	41	D3
Mirebeau	24	A2
Mirebeau	26	C3
Mirecourt	20	C2
Mirepoix	42	B2
Modane	33	D2
Modave	9	D3
Moirans	32	C2
Moirans-en-Montagne	27	D1
Moissac	35	F1
Mol	5	D2
Molières	35	F1
Moloy	26	C4
Molsheim	21	E3
Moncontour	15	D2
Mondorf-les-Bains	9	E1
Monestier-de-Clermont	32	C1
Monflanquin	35	E2
Monistrol-d'Allier	37	E3
Monistrol-sur-Loire	37	E4
Monnickendam	2	C1
Monpazier	35	E3
Monplaisir	24	B4
Mons (Bergen)	8	B3
Monségur	35	D2
Montagnac	43	D3
Montaigu	23	D2
Montaigu-de-Quercy	35	F2
Montaigut	30	C3
Montalivet	28	B1
Montaren	37	F1
Montargis	18	C1
Montastruc-la-Conseillère	42	A3
Montauban	41	F4
Montbard	26	B4
Montbazens	36	B2
Montbazon	24	B3
Montbéliard	27	F4
Montbenoît	27	E3
Montbonnot	32	C2
Montbrison	31	E1
Montbron	29	E2
Montbrun-les-Bains	38	C3
Montceau-les-Mines	26	B2
Montcornet	12	B3
Montcoutant	23	E1
Montcuq	35	F2
Mont-de-Marsan	40	C4
Montdidier	11	E1
Montdoubleau	24	B4
Montebourg	16	B4
Monte-Carlo	39	F2
Montélimar	38	A4
Montendre	34	C4
Montereau	18	C2
Montesquieu-Volvestre	41	F2
Montesquiou	41	D3
Montfaucon-en-Velay	37	F4
Montfort	15	E1
Montfort	18	A3
Montfort	40	B3
Montgenèvre	33	E1
Montgiscard	42	A3
Montguyon	35	D4
Montherme	12	C3
Monthois	12	C2
Monthureaux	20	C2

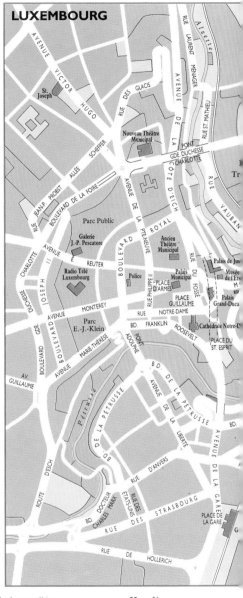

LUXEMBOURG

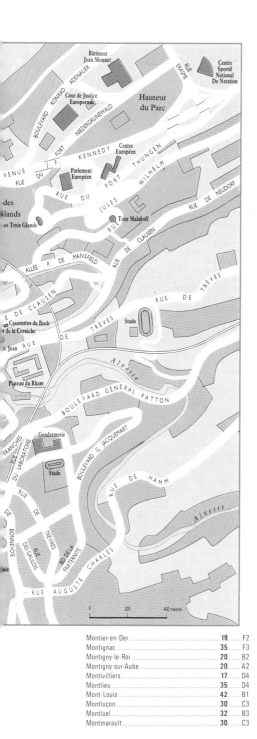

Bâtiment Jean Monnet

Centre Sportif National De Natation

BOULEVARD KONRAD ADENAUER

FORT NIEDERGRUNEWALD

Cour de Justice Europeenne

Hauteur du Parc

RUE ERASME

KENNEDY

Centre Européen

VENUE DU F.

Parlement Européen

RUE

FORT THUNGEN

RUE DU JULES WILHELM

des lands

es Trois Glands

Tour Malakoff

RUE DE NEUDORF

RUE DE CLAUSEN

ALLÉE P. DE MANSFIELD

RUE DE TREVES

RUE DE TREVES

E DE CLAUSEN

Casemates du Bock
de la Corniche

RUE DE

TREVES

Stade

t. Jean RUE DE

Plateau du Rham

Alzette

BOULEVARD GENERAL PATTON

VRANCHES

RUE DU LABORATOIRE

Gendarmerie

BOULEVARD G. JACQUEMART

RUE DE HAMM

Stade

RUE DE TREVIRES

RUE DE BONNEVOIE

DES GAULOIS

BD DE LA FRATERNITE

RUE AUGUSTE CHARLES

Alzette

ale

0   200   400 metres

Montmédy	**13**	D3
Montmélian	**32**	C3
Montmirail	**17**	E1
Montmirail	**19**	D3
Montmirey	**27**	D3
Montmoreau	**29**	D1
Montmorillon	**29**	E3
Montmort	**19**	D3
Montoire	**24**	B4
Montpellier	**43**	E3
Montpezat	**36**	A2
Montpon-Ménestérol	**35**	D3
Montpont	**26**	C2
Montréal	**42**	B2
Montréal	**41**	D4
Montréjeau	**41**	E2
Montrésor	**24**	B2
Montret	**26**	C2
Montreuil	**11**	D3
Montreuil-aux-Lions	**19**	D3
Montreuil-Bellay	**23**	F2
Montrevel	**26**	C1
Montrichard	**24**	B3
Montrod-les-Bains	**31**	E2
Montsalvy	**36**	C3
Montsauche	**26**	A3
Montsoreau	**23**	F2
Mont-sous-Vaudrey	**27**	D3
Monts-sur-Guesnes	**24**	A2
Montsûrs	**16**	C1
Morcenx	**34**	B1
Mordelles	**15**	E1
Morestel	**32**	B3
Moreuil	**11**	E1
Morez	**27**	D2
Morgat	**14**	A2
Morhange	**21**	D4
Morlaàs	**40**	C2
Morlaix	**14**	B3
Mormant	**18**	C2
Morosaglia	**44**	C3
Mortagne-au-Perche	**17**	E2
Mortagne-sur-Sèvre	**23**	D2
Mortain	**16**	B2
Morteau	**27**	E3
Mortrée	**17**	D2
Morzine	**33**	D4
Mouchard	**27**	D3
Mougins	**39**	E2
Mouliherne	**23**	F3
Moulins	**31**	D4
Moulins-Engilbert	**26**	A3
Moulins-la-Marche	**17**	E2
Moustiers-ste-Marie	**39**	D3
Mouthe	**27**	E2
Mouthier	**27**	E3
Mouthoumet	**42**	C2
Moutiers	**33**	D3
Moutiers	**28**	B4
Mouy	**18**	B4
Mouzon	**13**	D3
Mugron	**40**	C3
Mulhouse	**21**	E1
Munster	**21**	E2
Murat	**36**	C3
Murato	**44**	C3
Murat-sur-Vebre	**42**	C3
Mur-de-Barrez	**36**	C3
Mur-de-Bretagne	**14**	C2
Muret	**41**	F3
Muro	**44**	B3
Musselkanaal	**3**	F2

Montier-en-Der	**19**	F2
Montignac	**35**	F3
Montigny-le-Roi	**20**	B2
Montigny-sur-Aube	**20**	A2
Montivilliers	**17**	D4
Montlieu	**35**	D4
Mont-Louis	**42**	B1
Montluçon	**30**	C3
Montluel	**32**	B3
Montmarault	**30**	C3

Mussidan	**35**	E3
Mussy	**19**	F1
Muzillac	**22**	B3

N

Naarden	**5**	E4
Nadrin	**9**	D3
Nailloux	**42**	A3
Najac	**36**	B2
Nalzen	**42**	A2
Namur	**8**	C3
Nancy	**20**	C3
Nangis	**18**	C2
Nans-les-Pins	**38**	C2
Nant	**37**	D1
Nantes	**23**	D2
Nanteuil-le-Haudouin	**18**	C4
Nantiat	**29**	F2
Nantua	**32**	C4
Narbonne	**42**	C2
Narbonne-Plage	**43**	D2
Nasbinals	**37**	D2
Navarrenx	**40**	C2
Navilly	**26**	C2
Neede	**6**	B3
Nemours	**18**	C2
Nérac	**35**	D1
Néris-les-Bains	**30**	C3
Nérondes	**25**	E2
Nes	**3**	D3
Nesle	**11**	E1
Nettancourt	**20**	A3
Neuf-Brisach	**21**	E2
Neufchâteau	**20**	B2
Neufchâteau	**9**	D2
Neufchâtel	**12**	B2
Neufchâtel-en-Bray	**10**	C1
Neuillé Pont-Pierre	**24**	A3
Neuilly-l'Evêque	**20**	B1
Neuilly-St-Front	**12**	A2
Neu Moresnet	**9**	E4
Neung	**24**	C3
Neuves-Maisons	**20**	C3
Neuvic	**35**	E3
Neuvic	**36**	B4
Neuville	**24**	A2
Neuville	**32**	A3
Neuville-aux-Bois	**18**	B1
Neuvy	**30**	B4
Neuvy-sur-Barangeon	**25**	D3
Nevers	**25**	E2
Nexon	**29**	F2
Nice	**39**	F2
Niederbronn	**21**	E4
Nieppe	**11**	E3
Nieuil	**29**	E2
Nieuweschans	**3**	F3
Nieuwpoort	**4**	A2
Nijkerk	**5**	E4
Nijmegen	**5**	F3
Nijverdal	**6**	B4
Nîmes	**43**	F4
Ninove	**4**	C1
Niort	**28**	C3
Nitry	**26**	A4
Nivelles	**8**	B4

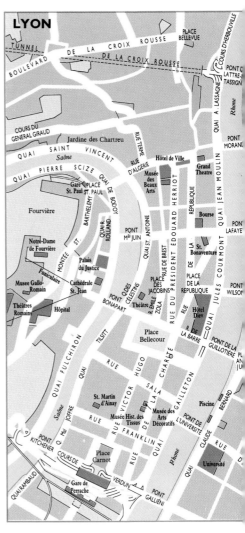

Noailles	**18**	B4
Nœux	**11**	E3
Nogaro	**41**	D3
Nogent	**20**	B2
Nogent-le-Roi	**18**	A3
Nogent-le-Rotrou	**17**	E1
Nogent-sur-Seine	**19**	D2
Noirétable	**31**	E2
Noirmoutier	**22**	B2
Nolay	**26**	B2
Nomeny	**20**	C4
Nomexy	**20**	C2
Nonancourt	**17**	F2
Nonant-le-Pin	**17**	D2
Nontron	**29**	E1
Nonza	**44**	C4
Noordwijk aan Zee	**5**	D4

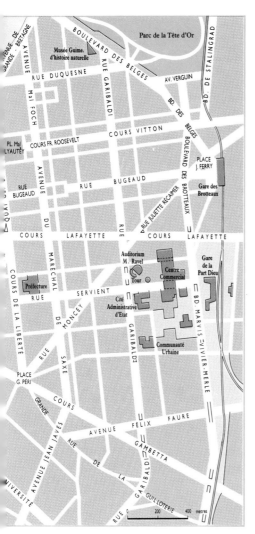

O

Obernai	**21**	E3
Oirschot	**5**	E2
Oisement	**11**	D2
Oisterwijk	**5**	E2
Olargues	**42**	C3
Oldenzaal	**6**	C4
Oletta	**44**	C3
Olette	**42**	B1
Olivet	**24**	C4
Olliergues	**31**	E2
Olmeto	**44**	B1
Olonzac	**42**	C2
Oloron-Ste-Marie	**40**	C2
Olst	**6**	B4
Ommen	**3**	E1
Onnaing	**12**	A4
Oostburg	**4**	B2
Oostehout	**5**	D3
Oostende	**4**	A2
Oosterbeek	**5**	F3
Oostérend	**2**	C3
Oosterwolde	**3**	E2
Oostmalle	**5**	D2
Ootmarsum	**3**	E1
Oraison	**38**	C3
Orange	**38**	B3
Orbec	**17**	E3
Orbey	**21**	E2
Orchies	**12**	A4
Orcières	**33**	D1
Orgelet	**27**	D2
Orgeval	**18**	B3
Orgon	**38**	B2
Orléans	**18**	B1
Orly	**18**	B3
Ornans	**27**	E3
Orthez	**40**	C3
Oss	**5**	E3
Otterlo	**5**	F4
Oucques	**24**	C4
Oud Beijerland	**4**	C3
Ouddorp	**4**	C3
Oudenaarde	**4**	B1
Oude-Pekela	**3**	F2
Ouistreham	**17**	D3
Oust	**41**	F1
Ouzouer-le-Marche	**18**	A1
Oyonnax	**27**	D1

Nordausques	**11**	D4
Norg	**3**	E2
Nort	**23**	D3
Nouan-le-Fuzelier	**25**	D3
Nouans-les-Fontaines	**24**	C2
Nouvion	**11**	D2
Noves	**38**	B3
Novion-Porcien	**12**	C3
Noyant	**23**	F3
Noyers	**26**	A4
Noyers-sur-Jabron	**38**	C3
Noyon	**11**	F1
Nozay	**22**	C3
Nozeroy	**27**	D2
Nuits-St-Georges	**26**	C3
Nunspeet	**3**	D1
Nyons	**38**	B4

P

Pacy-sur-Eure	**17**	F3
Pagny	**13**	E1
Paimbœuf	**22**	C3
Paimpol	**14**	C3
Paladru	**32**	C2
Palavas	**43**	E3
Paliseul	**8**	C2
Pamiers	**42**	A2
Panassac	**41**	E3
Paray-le-Monial	**31**	E3
Parentis-en-Born	**34**	B2
Paris	**18**	B3

Parthenay .... **29** D4
Partinello .... **44** B3
Pas de la Casa .... **42** A1
Pas-en-Artois .... **11** E2
Patay .... **18** A1
Pau .... **40** C2
Pauillac .... **34** C4
Paulhaguet .... **37** D4
Pavilly .... **10** B1
Payrac .... **36** A3
Péaule .... **22** B3
Peira-Cava .... **39** F3
Pellegrue .... **35** D3
Pentrez-Plage .... **14** A2
Percy .... **16** B3
Périers .... **16** B3
Périgueux .... **35** E4
Perkpolder .... **4** C2
Pernes .... **38** B3
Péronne .... **11** E2
Pérouges .... **32** B3
Perpignan .... **42** C1
Perros-Guirec .... **14** C3
Pertuis .... **38** C2
Péruwelz .... **8** A4
Pesmes .... **27** D3
Petange .... **9** D1
Petreto-Bicchisano .... **44** B2
Peyrat-le-Château .... **30** B2
Peyrehorade .... **40** B3
Peyrolles .... **38** C2
Peyruis .... **38** C3
Pézenas .... **43** D3
Phalsbourg .... **21** E3
Philippeville .... **8** B3
Piana .... **44** A3
Picquigny .... **11** D2
Piedicroce .... **44** C3
Pierre-Buffiere .... **30** A2
Pierre-de-Bresse .... **26** C2
Pierrefitte .... **20** B4
Pierrefitte-Nestalos .... **41** D2
Pierrefonds .... **18** C4
Pierrefort .... **36** C3
Pierrelatte .... **38** A4
Pierroton .... **34** C3
Pilat-Plage .... **34** B2
Piney .... **19** E2
Pino .... **44** C4
Pinols .... **37** D3
Pionsat .... **30** C3
Pipriac .... **22** C4
Piriac .... **22** B3
Pirou-Plage .... **16** B3
Pissos .... **34** C2
Pithiviers .... **18** B2
Plabennec .... **14** A2
Plaisance .... **41** D3
Plancoët .... **15** E2
Pleaux .... **36** B3
Plélan-le-Grand .... **15** E1
Plestin .... **14** C3
Pleumartin .... **24** B2
Pleyben .... **14** B2
Ploërmel .... **15** D1
Plombierès .... **21** D2
Plonéour Lanvern .... **14** A1
Plouaret .... **14** B3
Plouay .... **14** C1
Ploubalay .... **15** E2
Ploudalmezeau .... **14** A3
Plouescat .... **14** B3

MARSEILLE

Plougasnou .... **14** B3
Plouguenast .... **15** D2
Plouha .... **15** D3
Plouigneau .... **14** B3
Plouray .... **14** C2
Plozévet .... **14** A1
Pluvigner .... **22** A4
Podensac .... **34** C3
Poeldijk .... **4** C3
Pointe de Grave .... **28** B2

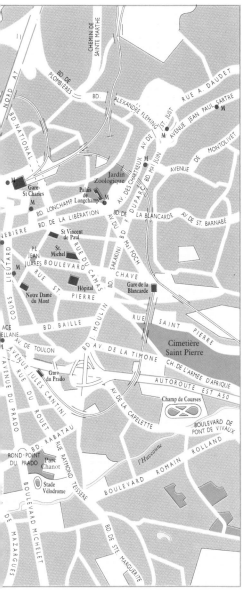

Pontacq	41	D2
Pontailler	26	C3
Pont-à-Mousson	20	C4
Pontarion	30	B2
Pontarlier	27	E2
Pontaubault	16	B2
Pont-Audemer	17	E3
Pontaumur	30	C2
Pont-Aven	14	B1
Pontcharra	32	C2
Pontchartrain	18	B3
Pontchâteau	22	C3
Pont-Croix	14	A1
Pont-d'Ain	32	B4
Pont-de-Briques	10	C3
Pont-de-Dore	31	D2
Pont-de-l'Arche	17	F3
Pont-de-Roide	27	F3
Pont de Salars	36	C2
Pont-de-Vaux	26	C1
Ponte-Leccia	44	B3
Pont-en-Royans	32	B2
Pontgibaud	30	C2
Pontigny	19	D1
Pontivy	14	C1
Pont-l'Abbe	14	A1
Pont-l'Evêque	17	D3
Pontlevoy	24	B3
Pontoise	18	B3
Pont-Réan	22	C4
Pontrieux	14	C3
Pont Scorff	22	A4
Pont-St-Esprit	38	A3
Pont-St-Vincent	20	C3
Pont-sur-Yonne	19	D2
Pontvallain	24	A4
Poperinge	4	A1
Pornic	22	C2
Pornichet	22	B3
Porquerolles	39	D1
Portbail	16	A4
Port-Barcarès	43	D1
Port Camargue	43	E3
Port-Cros	39	D1
Port-de-Bouc	38	B2
Port-en-Bessin	16	C4
Port Grimaud	39	E1
Porticcio	44	B2
Port-la-Nouvelle	43	D2
Port-Leucate	43	D2
Port-Louis	22	A4
Port-Manech	14	B1
Port-Navalo	22	A3
Porto	44	B3
Portorson	16	B2
Porto-Vecchio	44	C1
Port-Ste Marie	35	E2
Port-St-Louis-du-Rhône	38	B2
Port-sur-Saône	20	C1
Port-Vendres	43	D1
Pouancé	23	D3
Pougues-les-Eaux	25	E2
Pouilly	25	E3
Pouilly-en-Auxois	26	B3
Pouyastruc	41	D2
Pouzauges	23	E2
Pradelles	37	E3
Prades	42	C1
Prahecq	29	D3
Pralognan	33	E2
Prats-de-Mollo	42	C1
Prauthoy	26	C4
Pointe de Penmarch	14	A1
Pointe du Raz	14	A1
Poissons	20	B3
Poitiers	29	E4
Poix	11	D2
Poix-Terron	12	C3
Poligny	27	D2
Pompey	20	C3
Poncin	32	B4
Pons	28	C2

Précy-sous-Thil .... 26 ..... B3
Pré-en-Pail .... 17 ..... D2
Prémery .... 25 ..... F2
Pressac .... 29 ..... E3
Preuilly-sur-Claise .... 24 ..... B2
Primel-Trégastel .... 14 ..... B3
Privas .... 32 ..... A1
Profondeville .... 8 ..... C3
Propriano .... 44 ..... B1
Provins .... 19 ..... D2
Prunete-Cervione .... 44 ..... C3
Puget-sur-Argens .... 39 ..... E2
Puget-Théniers .... 39 ..... E3
Puget-Ville .... 39 ..... D1
Puiseaux .... 18 ..... B2
Puivert .... 42 ..... B2
Purmerend .... 2 ..... C1
Putanges .... 16 ..... C2
Puttelange .... 21 ..... D4
Putten .... 5 ..... E4
Puy de Dôme .... 30 ..... C2
Puy-Guillaume .... 31 ..... D2
Puylaurens .... 42 ..... B3
Puy-l'Evêque .... 35 ..... F2
Pyla-sur-Mer .... 34 ..... B3

Q

Quarré-le-Tombes .... 26 ..... A3
Questembert .... 22 ..... B3
Quettehou .... 16 ..... B4
Quiberon .... 22 ..... A3
Quillan .... 42 ..... B2
Quimper .... 14 ..... B1
Quimperle .... 14 ..... B1
Quinéville .... 16 ..... B4
Quingey .... 27 ..... D3
Quintin .... 15 ..... D2
Quissac .... 43 ..... E4

R

Raalte .... 6 ..... B4
Rabastens .... 42 ..... A4
Rabastens-de-Bigorre .... 41 ..... D3
Rambervillers .... 21 ..... D2
Rambouillet .... 18 ..... A3
Randan .... 31 ..... D2
Rânes .... 17 ..... D2
Raon-l'Etape .... 21 ..... D3
Raversijde .... 4 ..... A2
Rayol .... 39 ..... D1
Réalmont .... 42 ..... B3
Rebais .... 19 ..... D3
Recey-sur-Ource .... 20 ..... A1
Recologne .... 27 ..... D3
Redon .... 22 ..... C3
Reignier .... 33 ..... D4
Reims .... 12 ..... B2
Rémalard .... 17 ..... E1
Remich .... 9 ..... E1
Remiremont .... 21 ..... D2
Remouchamps .... 9 ..... D3
Remoulins .... 38 ..... A3
Rémuzat .... 38 ..... B4
Renaison .... 31 ..... E2
Renaix (Ronse) .... 4 ..... B1

NICE

Renkum .... 5 ..... E3
Rennes .... 15 ..... E1
Réquista .... 36 ..... C1
Ressons .... 11 ..... E1
Rethel .... 12 ..... C2
Retiers .... 23 ..... D4
Retournac .... 37 ..... E4
Reuilly .... 25 ..... D2
Reusel .... 5 ..... D2
Revel .... 42 ..... B3
Révigny .... 20 ..... A3
Revin .... 12 ..... C3
Rhenen .... 5 ..... E3
Rhinau .... 21 ..... E2
Riaillé .... 23 ..... D3
Rians .... 38 ..... C2
Ribeauville .... 21 ..... E2
Ribécourt .... 11 ..... E1

Ribemont

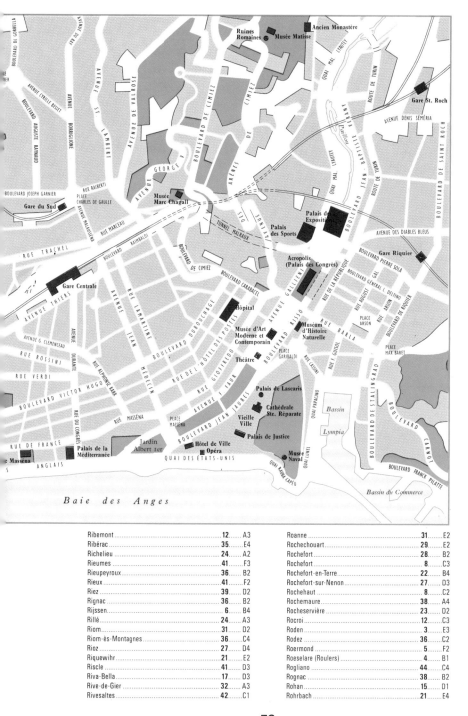

Ruines Romaines · Musée Matisse · Ancien Monastère · Gare St. Roch · Avenue Denis Séméria · Boulevard de Saint Roch · Boulevard de Gorbella · Avenue du Ray · Avenue Cyrille Besset · Boulevard Auguste Raynaud · Boulevard Borriglione · Avenue de Valrose · Avenue St. Lambert · Avenue de Cimiez · Cimiez · Arènes de · Quai Mal. Lyautey · Quai Mal. Lyautey · Quai du Turin · Route de Turin · Boulevard Jean Baptiste Vérany · George V · Route de Turin · Avenue des Diables Bleus · Boulevard Joseph Garnier · Rue Raiberti · Place Charles de Gaulle · Avenue Malaussena · Musée Marc Chagall · Palais des Expositions · Gare du Sud · Rue Marceau · Tunnel Malraux · Palais des Sports · Palais des Congrès · Gare Riquier · Boulevard Pierre Sola · Boulevard Raimbaldi · Boulevard de Cimiez · Acropolis (Palais des Congrès) · Rue de la République · Boulevard Général L. Delfino · Rue Rue Trachel · Gare Centrale · Avenue Thiers · Avenue Jean Médecin · Rue Lamartine · Boulevard Carabacel · Rue Auguste Gal · Place Arson · Rue de Riquier · Avenue G. Clemenceau · Avenue Durante · Rue Alphonse Karr · Boulevard Dubouchage · Avenue Galliéni · Rue Rossi · Rue J. Gubiol · Place Max Baret · Hôpital · Avenue Rue Rue Barla · Rue Rossini · Rue Verdi · Rue de l'Hôtel des Postes · Musée d'Art Moderne et Contemporain · Muséum d'Histoire Naturelle · Rue Cassini · Boulevard Victor Hugo · Rue Gioffredo · Place Garibaldi · Théâtre · Rue du Congrès · Rue Masséna · Avenue F. Faur · Avenue Jean Jaurès · Palais de Lascaris · Bassin · Boulevard de Stalingrad · Boulevard Carnot · Rue de France · Place Masséna · Vieille Ville · Cathédrale Ste. Réparate · Quai Papacino · Lympia · Palais de la Méditerranée · Jardin Albert 1er · Hôtel de Ville · Opéra · Palais de Justice · Quai Lunel · Musée Naval · Quai Rauba Capeu · Boulevard Franck Pilatte · Masséna · Anglais · Quai des États-Unis · Bassin du Commerce

Baie des Anges

Ribemont	**12**	A3	Roanne	**31**	E2
Ribérac	**35**	E4	Rochechouart	**29**	E2
Richelieu	**24**	A2	Rochefort	**28**	B2
Rieumes	**41**	F3	Rochefort	**8**	C3
Rieupeyroux	**36**	B2	Rochefort-en-Terre	**22**	B4
Rieux	**41**	F2	Rochefort-sur-Nenon	**27**	D3
Riez	**39**	D2	Rochehaut	**8**	C2
Rignac	**36**	B2	Rochemaure	**38**	A4
Rijssen	**6**	B4	Rocheservière	**23**	D2
Rillé	**24**	A3	Rocroi	**12**	C3
Riom	**31**	D2	Roden	**3**	E3
Riom-ès-Montagnes	**36**	C4	Rodez	**36**	C2
Rioz	**27**	D4	Roermond	**5**	F2
Riquewihr	**21**	E2	Roeselare (Roulers)	**4**	B1
Riscle	**41**	D3	Rogliano	**44**	C4
Riva-Bella	**17**	D3	Rognac	**38**	B2
Rive-de-Gier	**32**	A3	Rohan	**15**	D1
Rivesaltes	**42**	C1	Rohrbach	**21**	E4

Roisel	11	F2
Romans-sur-Isère	32	B2
Rombas	13	E2
Romilly-sur-Seine	19	D2
Romorantin-Lanthenay	24	C3
Ronchamp	21	D1
Ronse (Renaix)	4	B1
Roodeschool	3	E3
Roosendaal	5	D2
Roquebilliere	39	F3
Roquebrune-Cap-Martin	39	F2
Roquefort	34	C1
Roquefort-sur-Soulzon	42	C4
Rosans	38	C4
Roscoff	14	B3
Rosporden	14	B1
Rostassac	35	F2
Rostrenen	14	C2
Rothéneuf	15	E3
Rotterdam	5	D3
Roubaix	11	F3
Rouen	17	F4
Rouffach	21	E2
Rouge	23	D4
Rougemont	21	D1
Rougemont	27	E4
Rouillac	29	D2
Roujan	43	D3
Roulers (Roeselare)	4	B1
Roussillon	38	B3
Rouvres-en-Xaintois	20	C2
Royan	28	B2
Royat	31	D2
Roybon	32	B2
Roye	11	E1
Royère	30	B2
Rozay-en-Brie	18	C3
Rozoy	12	B3
Rue	11	D3
Ruelle	29	D2
Ruffec	29	D2
Ruffieux	32	C3
Rugles	17	E2
Rumigny	12	C3
Rumilly	32	C3
Rupt	21	D2
Ruurlo	6	B3

S

Saales	21	E2
Sables-d'Or	15	D3
Sablé-sur-Sarthe	23	F4
Sabres	34	C1
Saeul	9	D2
Sagone	44	B2
Saillagouse	42	B1
Saillans	32	B1
Sains	12	B3
Sainte Anne-d'Auray	22	A4
Sainte Anne-la-Palud	14	A2
Sainte Croix-Volvestre	41	F2
Sainte Enimie	37	D2
Sainte Foy-la-Grande	35	D3
Sainte Gauburge-Sainte Colombe	17	E2
Sainte Hélène	34	C3
Sainte Hermine	28	B4
Sainte Marie-aux-Mines	21	E2
Sainte Marie-de-Campan	41	D2
Sainte Maries-de-la-Mer	43	F3
Sainte Maure-de-Touraine	24	A2
Sainte Maxime	39	E1
Sainte Menehould	13	D2
Sainte Mère-Église	16	B4
Saintes	28	C2
Sainte Sévère	30	B3
Sainte Suzanne	23	F4

PARIS

Sainte Tulle	**38**	C2
Saissac	**42**	B2
Salbris	**25**	D3
Salernes	**39**	D2
Salers	**36**	C3
Salies-de-Béarn	**40**	B3
Salies-du-Salat	**41**	E2
Salignac-Eyvignes	**35**	F3
Salins	**27**	D2
Sallanches	**33**	D4
Salles	**34**	B2
Salles	**42**	A2
Salles-Curan	**36**	C1
Salon	**19**	E3
Salon-de-Provence	**38**	E3
Salses	**42**	C1
Salviac	**35**	F3
Samadet	**40**	C3
Samatan	**41**	E3
Samer	**11**	D3

75

Samoëns	33	D4
Sanary	38	C1
Sancergues	25	E2
Sancerre	25	E3
Sancoins	25	E2
Sanguinet	34	B2
Santa Maria-Siche	44	B2
Santa Severa	44	C4
Sappemeer	3	E3
Saramon	41	E3
Sarlat-la-Canéda	35	F3
Sarralbe	21	D4
Sarrebourg	21	D3
Sarreguemines	21	D4
Sarre-Union	21	D4
Sarron	40	C3
Sartène	44	B1
Sartilly	16	B2
Sarzeau	22	B3
Sassenage	32	C2
Sassenheim	5	D4
Saucats	34	C3
Saugues	37	D3
Saujon	28	C2
Saulieu	26	B3
Sault	38	C3
Saulx	20	C1
Saulxures	21	D2
Saumur	23	F2
Sauve	43	E4
Sauveterre-de-Béarn	40	B3
Sauveterre-de-Guyenne	35	D3
Sauxillanges	31	D1
Sauzé-Vaussais	29	D3
Sauzon	22	A3
Savenay	22	C3
Saverdun	42	A2
Saverne	21	E3
Savignac-les-Eglises	35	E4
Savigny-sur-Braye	24	B4
Savines-le-Lac	39	D4
Scaër	14	B1
Schagen	2	C2
Scheveningen	4	C4
Schiermonnikoog	3	D3
Schilde	5	D2
Schirmeck	21	E3
Schoondijke	4	B2
Schoonebeek	3	E1
Schoonhoven	5	D3
Schoonoord	3	E2
Seclin	11	F3
Secondigny	28	C4
Sedan	13	D3
Séderon	38	C3
Sées	17	D2
Segonzac	29	D2
Segré	23	E3
Seiches	23	E3
Seilhac	36	A4
Sélestat	21	E2
Selles	24	C3
Sellières	27	D2
Selongey	26	C4
Seltz	21	F4
Semur-en-Auxois	26	B4
Sénas	38	B2
Senlis	18	C4
Sennecey-le-Grand	26	C2
Senonches	17	E2
Senones	21	D3
Sens	19	D2
Sept-Saulx	12	C2
Seraing	9	D4
Sérent	22	B4
Sermaize-les-Bains	20	A3
Serres	38	C4
Serrières	32	A2
Sète	43	E3
Seurre	26	C3
Sévérac-le-Château	37	D2
Sevrier	33	D3
Seyches	35	D2
Seyne	39	D4
Seyssel	32	C4
Sézanne	19	D3
's Heerenberg	6	B3
Sierck	13	F2
Sierentz	21	E1
Sigean	42	C2
Signy-l'Abbaye	12	C3
Sillé-le-Guillaume	17	D1
Siorac-en-Périgord	35	F3
Sisteron	38	C3
Sittard	5	F1
Six-Fours	38	C1
Sizun	14	B2
Sliedrecht	5	D3
Sloten	3	D2

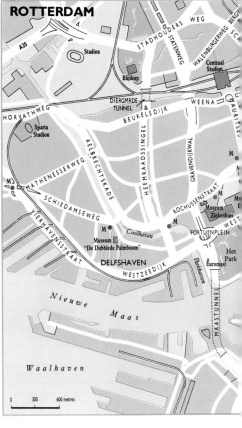

Sluis

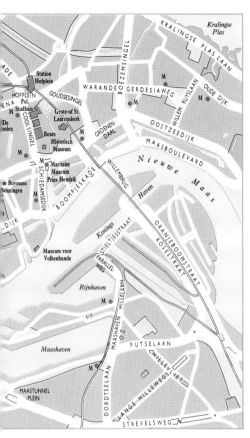

Station Hofplein
HOFPLEIN Pol.
Stadhuis
Grote-of St. Laurenskerk
Beurs
Historisch Museum
Mariteim Museum
Prins Hendrik
Boymans Beuningen
Museum voor Volkenhunde
KRALINGSE PLAS LAAN
Kralingse Plas
WARANDE GERDESIAWEG
GOUDSESINGEL
BOEZEMSINGEL
WILLEM RUYSLAAN
OUDE DIJK
GROENEN DAAL
OOSTZEEDIJK
MAASBOULEVARD
Nieuwe Maas
SCHIEDAMSEDIJK
WILLEMBRUG
BOOMPJESKADE
Haven
Konings
STIELTIESSTRAAT
ORANJEBOOMSTRAAT
ROSESTRAAT
PARALLEL WEG
Rijnhaven
Maashaven
MAASHAVEN OZ
HILLELAAN
PUTSELAAN
DORDTSELAAN
CHILLEVLIET
LANGE HILLEWEG
HET
MAASTUNNEL -PLEIN
STREVELSWEG

Sluis	4	B2
Sluis	4	C3
Smilde	3	E2
Sneek	3	D2
Soest	5	E4
Soestdijk	5	E4
Soignies	8	B4
Soissons	12	A2
Solenzara	44	C2
Solliès-Pont	39	D1
Sombernon	26	B3
Sommesous	19	E3
Sommières	43	E3
Sore	34	C2
Sospel	39	F3
Sotta	44	B1
Souesmes	25	D3
Soufflenheim	21	F4
Souillac	36	A3
Souilly	13	D1
Soulac	28	B1
Soultz	21	E1
Soultz	21	F4
Soumoulou	41	D2
Souppes	18	C2
Sourdeval	16	B2
Sousceyrac	36	B3

Soustons	40	B3
Souvigny	31	D3
Spa	9	D3
Spakenburg	5	E4
Spijkenisse	4	C3
Spincourt	13	E2
St Abbs	34	C4
St Affrique	42	C4
St Agnant	28	B2
St Agrève	37	F3
St Aignan	24	C3
St Aignan	23	D4
St Aignan	33	G4
St Alban	37	D3
St Amand-en-Puisaye	25	E3
St Amand-les-Eaux	12	A4
St Amand Longpré	24	B4
St Amans	37	D2
St Amant-Roche-Savine	31	D1
St Ambroix	37	E2
St Amé	21	D2
St Amour	26	C1
St André	17	F2
St André-du-Cubzac	34	C3
St André-les-Alpes	39	D3
St Annaparochie	3	D3
St Anthème	31	E1
St Antonin-Noble-Val	36	A1
St Armand-Montrond	25	D2
St Aubin-d'Aubigné	16	A1
St Aubin-du-Cormier	16	B1
St Aubin-sur-Mer	16	C3
St Aulaye	35	D4
St Avold	13	F2
St Aygulf	39	E2
St Bard Maison Rouge	30	C2
St Béat	41	E2
St Beauzély	36	C1
St Benin	25	F2
St Benoît	30	A3
St Benoit-sur-Loire	25	D4
St Bertrand-de-Comminges	41	E2
St Blin	20	B2
St Bonnet	33	D1
St Bonnet de Joux	31	F3
St Bonnet-le-Chateau	31	E1
St Brévin	22	C2
St Brice-en-Coglès	16	B2
St Brieuc	15	D2
St Calais	24	B4
St Cast	15	E3
St Céré	36	B3
St Cernin	36	B3
St Chamas	38	B2
St Chamond	31	F1
St Chély-d'Apcher	37	D3
St Chely-d'Aubrac	36	C2
St Chinian	42	C3
St Ciers	34	C4
St Clar	41	E4
St Claud	29	E2
St Claude	27	D1
St Cyprien	35	F3
St Cyprien-Plage	43	D1
St Denis	18	B3
St Denis d'Oléron	28	B3
St Denis d'Orques	23	F4
St Didier-en-Velay	37	F4
St Dié	21	D2
St Dizier	20	A3
St Donat-sur-l'Herbasse	32	B2
St Emilion	35	D3

St Etienne	31	F1
St Etienne	38	C3
St Etienne-de-Baigory	40	B2
St Etienne-de-St-Geoirs	32	B2
St Etienne-de-Tinée	39	E3
St Fargeau	25	E3
St Firmin	32	C1
St Florent	23	D3
St Florent	25	D2
St Florent	44	C3
St Florentin	19	D1
St Flour	37	D3
St Fulgent	23	D2
St Galmier	31	F1
St Gaudens	41	E2
St Gaultier	24	C1
St Geniez-d'Olt	36	C2
St Genis-de-Saintonge	28	C1
St Genix	32	C3
St Georges	23	E3
St Georges-de-Didonne	28	B2
St Geours-de-Maremne	40	B3
St Germain	18	B3
St Germain	30	A2
St Germain-de-Joux	32	C4
St Germain-des-Vaux	16	A4
St Germain-du-Bois	26	C2
St Germain-du-Plain	26	C2
St Germain-Laval	31	E2
St Germain-Lembron	31	D1
St Germain-l'Herm	31	D1
St Germain-Plage	16	A3
St Gervais	33	D3
St Gervais	43	D3
St Gervais-d'Auvergne	30	C2
St Géry	36	A2
St Gildas-des-Bois	22	C3
St Gilles	43	F3
St Gilles-Croix-de-Vie	22	C1
St Giron-Plage	40	B4
St Girons	41	F2
St Gorgan-Main	27	E3
St Guénolé	14	A1
St Hilaire-de-Villefranche	28	C2
St Hilaire-du-Harcouët	16	B2
St Hippolyte	27	F3
St Hippolyte-du-Fort	43	E4
St Honoré	26	A2
St Hubert	9	D2
St Jacut	15	E2
St James	16	B2
St Jean-Brévelay	22	B4
St Jean-Cap-Ferrat	39	F2
St Jean-d'Angély	28	C2
St Jean-de-Bournay	32	B3
St Jean-de-Losne	26	C3
St Jean-de-Luz	40	A3
St Jean-de-Maurienne	33	D2
St Jean-de-Monts	22	C2
St Jean du Bruel	37	D1
St Jean du Gard	37	E1
St Jean-le-Thomas	16	B2
St Jean-Pied-de-Port	40	B2
St Jeoire	33	D4
St Jorioz	33	D3
St Jouan-de-l'Isle	15	E2
St Julien-Chapteuil	37	E3
St Julien-de-Vouvantes	23	D3
St Julien-en-Beauchêne	38	C4
St Julien-en-Genevois	32	C4
St Julien-l'Ars	29	E4
St Junien	29	E2

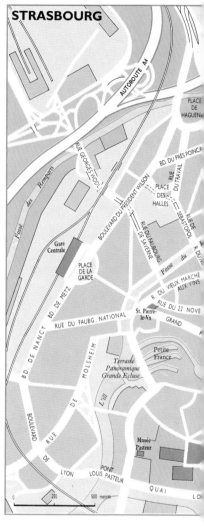

STRASBOURG

St Just-en-Chaussée	11	E1
St Just-en-Chevalet	31	E2
St Justin	41	D4
St Lary-Soulan	41	D1
St Laurent	16	C4
St Laurent	29	F2
St Laurent-en-Grandvaux	27	D2
St Laurent-et-Benon	34	C4
St Leger	26	A2
St Léonard-de-Noblat	30	A2
St Lô	16	B3
St Louis	21	E1
St Loup-sur-Semouse	20	C1
St Lunaire	15	E3
St Lys	41	F3
St Macaire	35	D2
St Maclou	17	E3

St Maixent-l'Ecole

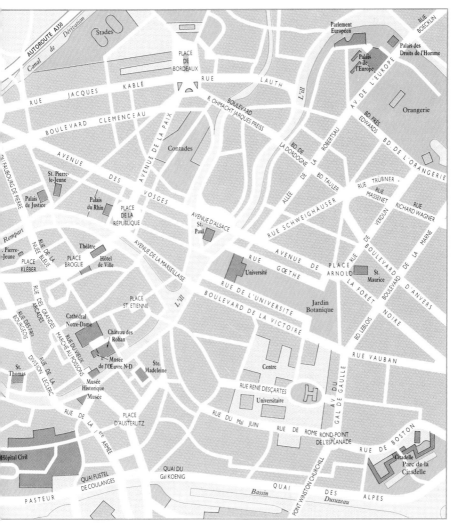

St Maixent-l'Ecolye	29	D3
St Malo	15	E3
St Marcellin	32	B2
St Mars-la-Jaille	23	D3
St Martin-d'Auxigny	25	D3
St Martin-de-Londres	43	E3
St Martin-de-Ré	28	B3
St Martin-Vésubie	39	F3
St Martory	41	E2
St Mathieu	29	E2
St Maurice-sur-Moselle	21	D1
St Maximin-la-Sainte-Baume	38	C2
St Méen	15	E2
St Michel-de-Maurienne	33	D2
St Michel-en-Greve	14	C3
St Michel-en-l'Herm	28	B3
St Mihiel	20	B4
St Nazaire	22	C3
St Nectaire	30	C1
St Nicolas	22	C3
St Nicolas-de-Port	20	C3
St Nicolas-du-Pélem	14	C2
St Niklaas	4	C2
St Oedenrode	5	E2
St Omer	11	D4
St Palais	40	B2
St Palais-sur-Mer	28	B2
St Pardoux-la-Rivière	29	E1
St Paul	39	E4
St Paul	39	E2
St Paul-Cap-de-Joux	42	B3
St Paul-de-Fenouillet	42	C1
St Pauliene	37	C3
St Pé	41	D2

St Péray	32	A1
St Père-en-Retz	22	C2
St Philbert	22	C2
St Pierre-d'Albigny	33	D3
St Pierre-de-Chartreuse	32	C2
St Pierre-de-Chignac	35	E3
St Pierre-d'Oléron	28	B2
St Pierre-Église	16	B4
St Pierre-le-Moûtier	25	E2
St Pierre-Quiberon	22	A3
St Pierre-sur-Dives	17	D3
St Pois	16	B2
St Pol-de-Léon	14	B3
St Pol-sur-Ternoise	11	E3
St Pons	42	C3
St Porchaire	28	C2
St Pourcain	31	D3
St Privat	36	B3
St Quay-Portrieux	15	D3
St Quentin	12	A3
St Rambert-d'Albon	32	A2
St Rambert-en-Bugey	32	B3
St Raphael	39	E2
St Rémy-de-Provence	38	B2
St Renan	14	A2
St Riquier	11	D2
St Rome-de-Tarn	36	C1
St Saëns	10	C1
St Satur	25	E3
St Saulge	25	F2
St Sauvant	29	D3
St Sauveur-en-Puisaye	25	F4
St Sauveur-le-Vicomte	16	B4
St Sauveur-sur-Tiné	39	E3
St Savin	29	E4
St Savin	34	C4
St Seine-l'Abbaye	26	B3
St Sernin-sur-Rance	42	C4
St Sever	16	B2
St Sever	40	C3
St Symphorien	34	C2
St Symphorien-de Lay	31	E2
St Symphorien-d'Ozon	32	B3
St Symphorien-sur-Coise	31	F2
St Thiébault	20	B2
St Trivier-de-Courtes	26	C1
St Tropez	39	D1
St Truiden	5	E1
St Vaast-la-Hougue	16	B4
St Valery-en-Caux	10	B2
St Valery-sur-Somme	11	D2
St Vallier-de-Thiey	39	E2
St Vallier-sur-Rhône	32	A2
St Vaury	30	B3
St Véran	33	E1
St Vincent-de-Tyrosse	40	B3
St Vith	9	E3
St Vivien-de-Médoc	28	B1
St Yrieix-la-Perche	29	F1
Stadskanaal	3	F2
Stainville	20	B3
Stavelot	9	D3
Stavenisse	4	C3
Staveren	2	C2
Steenbergen	4	C3
Steenvoorde	11	E4
Steenwijk	3	D2
Stellendam	4	C3
Stenay	13	D2
Stiens	3	D3
Strasbourg	21	E3
Suippes	12	C2
Sully	25	D4
Surgères	28	C3
Survilliers	18	C4
Swalmen	5	F2

T

Tain-l'Hermitage	32	A2
Tallard	39	D4
Talloires	33	D3
Talmont	28	C1
Talmont-St-Hilaire	28	A3
Tancarville	17	E4
Taninges	33	D4
Tarare	31	F2
Tarascon	38	A2
Tarascon-sur-Ariège	42	A1
Tarbes	41	D2
Tardets-Sorholus	40	B2
Tarnos	40	A3
Tartas	40	B4
Tauves	30	C1
Tavaux	26	C3
Tavernes	39	D2
Tegelen	5	F2
Temse	4	C2
Tence	37	F3
Tende	39	F3
Ter Apel	3	F2
Terneuzen	4	C2
Terrasson-la-Villedieu	35	F3
Tervuren	5	D1
Tessy	16	B3
Thann	21	E1
Thénezay	23	F1
Thenon	35	F3
Théoule	39	E2
Thérouanne	11	D3
Theux	9	D3
Thiaucourt	13	E1
Thiberville	17	E3
Thiéblemont-Farémont	19	F3
Thiers	31	D2
Thionville	13	E2
Thivars	17	F1
Thiviers	29	E1
Thizy	31	F2
Thoissey	32	A4
Thonon	27	E1
Thouarce	23	E2
Thouars	23	F2
Thueyts	37	E2
Thuir	42	C1
Thury-Harcourt	16	C3
Tiel	5	E3
Tielt	4	B1
Tienen	5	D1
Tierce	23	E3
Tignes	33	E3
Tilburg	5	D2
Til-Châtel	26	C4
Tinchebray	16	C2
Tongeren (Tongres)	5	E1
Tongres (Tongeren)	5	E1
Tonnay-Boutonne	28	C2
Tonnay-Charente	28	C2
Tonneins	35	D2
Tonnerre	19	E1
Torhout	4	A2

Torigni	16	B3
Tôtes	10	C1
Toucy	25	F4
Toul	20	C3
Toulon	38	C1
Toulon-sur-Arroux	26	A2
Toulouse	42	A3
Tourcoing	11	F3
Tournai (Doornik)	8	A4
Tournan	18	C3
Tournay	41	D2
Tournon	32	A2
Tournon-d'Agenais	35	F2
Tournon-St-Martin	24	B2
Tournus	26	C2
Tours	24	B3
Toury	18	B2
Trébeurden	14	C3
Tréboul	14	A2
Trégastel	14	C3
Tréguier	14	C3
Treignac	30	B1
Trets	38	C2
Trévoux	32	A3
Triaize	28	B3
Triaucourt	13	D1
Trie	41	D2
Troarn	17	D3
Trois-Ponts	9	D3
Trouville	17	D3
Troyes	19	E2
Truchtersheim	21	E3
Trun	17	D2
Tuchan	42	C2
Tuffe	17	E1
Tulle	36	A4
Tullins	32	C2
Turckheim	21	E2
Turnhout	5	D2
Tzummarum	3	D3

U

Uckange	13	E2
Uden	5	E3
Ugine	33	D3
Uithoorn	5	D4
Uithuizen	3	E3
Urdos	40	C1
Urk	3	D2
Ury	18	C2
Ussel	30	B1
Ustaritz	40	A3
Utrecht	5	E4
Uzel	15	D2
Uzerche	30	A1
Uzès	37	F1

V

Vaas	24	A4
Vaassen	6	A4
Vaiges	23	E4
Vailly	12	A2
Vailly	25	E3
Vaison-la-Romaine	38	B3

Valberg	39	E3
Valbonnais	32	C1
Val-Claret	33	E2
Valdahon	27	E3
Val d'Esquières	39	E1
Val d'Isére	33	E3
Valençay	24	C2
Valence	32	B1
Valence	35	E1
Valence	41	E4
Valence d'Albigeois	36	B1
Valenciennes	12	A4
Valensole	39	D3
Valkenburg	5	F1
Valkenswaard	5	E2
Valleraugue	37	E1
Vallet	23	D2
Valloire	33	D2
Vallon en Sully	30	C3
Vallon-Pont-d'Arc	37	F2
Vallorcine	33	E4
Vallouise	33	D1
Valmorel	33	D2
Valognes	16	B4
Valras-Plage	43	D2
Valréas	38	B4
Vals-les-Bains	37	F2
Val-Suzon	26	C3
Vannes	22	B3
Varades	23	D3
Varces	32	C2
Varengeville	10	C2
Varennes-en-Argonne	13	D2
Varennes-sur-Allier	31	D3
Varilhes	42	A2
Vars	39	E4
Varsseveld	6	B3
Varzy	25	F3
Vassy	16	C2
Vatan	24	C2
Vaucouleurs	20	B3
Vauvert	43	F3
Vauville	16	A4
Vauvillers	20	C2
Vayrac	36	A3
Veendam	3	E3
Veenendaal	5	E3
Veere	4	B3
Veghel	5	E3
Veldhoven	5	E2
Velp	6	A3
Venaco	44	B3
Vence	39	E2
Vendargues	43	E3
Vendeuvre	19	E2
Vendôme	24	B4
Venlo	5	F2
Venray	5	F2
Verberie	18	C4
Verdun	13	D2
Verfeil	42	A3
Vergt	35	E3
Vermenton	26	A4
Vernet	42	A3
Vernet-les-Bains	42	B1
Verneuil	17	E2
Vernon	18	A4
Verny	13	F1
Versailles	18	B3
Verteillac	35	E4
Vertus	19	E3
Verviers	9	D4

Vervins	12	B3
Verzy	12	B2
Vesoul	27	E4
Veules-les-Roses	10	B2
Veulettes-sur-Mer	10	B2
Veurne (Furnès)	4	A2
Veynes	38	C4
Veyrier	33	D3
Vézelay	26	A4
Vézelise	20	C3
Vézénobres	37	E1
Viais	23	D2
Vianden	9	E2
Vianen	5	D3
Vianne	35	D2
Vias	43	D2
Vibraye	24	B4
Vic	31	D2
Vicdessos	42	A1
Vic-en-Bigorre	41	D3
Vic-Fezensac	41	D3
Vichy	31	D3
Vico	44	B2
Vic-sur-Aisne	18	C4
Vic-sur-Cère	36	C3
Vidauban	39	D2
Vielsalm	9	D3
Vienne	32	B3
Vierzon	25	D3
Vieux-Boucau	40	B3
Vif	32	C2
Vigneulles	13	E1
Vignory	20	A2
Vihiers	23	E2
Villaines-la-Juhel	16	C1
Villandraut	34	C2
Villandry	24	A2
Villard-de-lans	32	C2
Villars	27	E3
Villars	39	E3
Villars-les-Dombes	32	B4
Villé	21	E3
Villebois Lavalette	29	D1
Villedieu-les-Poêles	16	B3
Ville-en-Tardenois	12	B2
Villefagnan	29	D2
Villefort	37	E2
Villefranche	39	F2
Villefranche-d'Albigeois	42	B4
Villefranche-de-Lauragais	42	A3
Villefranche-de-Lonchat	35	D3
Villefranche-de-Rouergue	36	B2
Villefranche-du-Périgord	35	F2
Villefranche-sur-Cher	24	C3
Villefranche-sur-Saone	32	A4
Villemur	42	A4
Villenauxe-la-Grande	19	D2
Villeneuve	36	B2
Villeneuve	38	A3
Villeneuve-de-Berg	37	F2
Villeneuve-de-Marsan	40	C4
Villeneuve-l'Archevêque	19	D2
Villeneuve-Loubet	39	E2
Villeneuve-sur-Allier	25	F1
Villeneuve-sur-Lot	35	E2
Villeneuve-sur-Yonne	19	D1
Villeréal	35	E2
Villers	17	D3
Villers Bocage	16	C3
Villers-Bretonneux	11	E2
Villers-Cotterêts	18	C4
Villersexel	27	E4
Villers-St.Georges	19	D3
Villerville	17	D4
Vimoutiers	17	D4
Vinay	32	B2
Vinca	42	C1
Vinon-sur-Verdon	38	C2
Vire	16	C2
Virieu	32	C3
Virieu-le-Grand	32	C3
Virton	9	D1
Visé	9	D4
Vitré	16	B1
Vitry-le-François	19	F3
Vitteaux	26	B3
Vittel	20	C2
Vivario	44	B2
Viviers	38	A4
Vivonne	29	D3
Vizille	32	C2
Vizzavona	44	B2
Vlaardingen	4	C3
Vlagtweede	3	F2
Vlissingen	4	B2
Void	20	B3
Voiron	32	C2
Voise	18	A2
Voix	38	C3
Volendam	2	C1
Voorschoten	5	D4
Voorst	6	B4
Voreppe	32	C2
Vorey	37	E4
Vouillé	29	D4
Vouvray	24	B4
Vouziers	12	C2
Voves	18	A2
Vresse	8	C2
Vron	11	D3
Vroomshoop	3	E1
Vught	5	E3

W

Waalwijk	5	D3
Wageningen	5	E3
Wangenbourg	21	E3
Waregem	4	B1
Waremme	8	C4
Warnsveld	6	B4
Wasselone	21	E3
Wassenaar	4	C4
Wasserbillig	9	E2
Wassy	20	A3
Waterloo	8	B4
Waulsort	8	C3
Wavre	8	C4
Weert	5	E2
Well	5	F2
Wellin	8	C3
Wemperhaardt	9	E3
Wépion	8	C3
Werbomont	9	D3
Westende-Bad	4	A2
Westerlo	5	D1
Westkapelle	4	B2
West-Terchelling	2	C3
Wetteren	4	C1
Wierden	6	B4
Wijhe	6	B4

Willebroek .... **4** C1
Willemstad .... **5** D3
Wiltz .... **9** D2
Wimereux .... **11** D4
Winschoten .... **3** F3
Winsum .... **3** E3
Winterswijk .... **6** B3
Wissant .... **11** D4
Wissembourg .... **21** F4
Woerden .... **5** D4
Wœrth .... **21** E4
Wolvega .... **3** D2
Workum .... **2** C2
Wormerveer .... **2** B1
Wormhout .... **11** E4
Wuustwezel .... **5** D2

X

Xertigny .... **21** D2
Xhoffraix .... **9** E3

Y

Yenne .... **32** C3
Yerville .... **10** B1
Yport .... **10** B1
Ypres (Ieper) .... **4** A1
Yssingeaux .... **37** E3
Yvetot .... **10** B1
Yvoir .... **8** C3
Yvoire .... **27** E1

Z

Zaandam .... **2** B1
Zaltbommel .... **5** E3
Zandvoort .... **2** B1
Zeebrugge .... **4** B2
Zeist .... **5** E4
Zelzate .... **4** C2
Zevenaar .... **6** A3
Zevenergen .... **5** D3
Zicavo .... **44** B2
Zierikzee .... **4** C3
Zijpe .... **4** C3
Zoetermeer .... **5** D4
Zolder .... **5** E1
Zonza .... **44** B1
Zoutkamp .... **3** E3
Zuidhorn .... **3** E3
Zuidlaren .... **3** E2
Zundert .... **5** D2
Zutphen .... **6** B4
Zwijindrecht .... **5** D3
Zwolle .... **3** D1

Distance chart
(kilometres)

Diagonal city labels (1–42):

1 Amsterdam
2 Antwerpen
3 Biarritz
4 Bordeaux
5 Boulogne-sur-Mer
6 Brussel
7 Caen
8 Calais
9 Cherbourg
10 Clermont-Ferrand
11 Dieppe
12 Dijon
13 Dunkerque
14 Grenoble
15 Groningen
16 Den Haag
17 Le Havre
18 Liège
19 Lille
20 Limoges
21 Luxembourg
22 Lyon
23 Le Mans
24 Marseille
25 Nantes
26 Nice
27 Oostende
28 Orleans
29 Paris
30 Perpignan
31 Quimper
32 Reims
33 La Rochelle
34 Roscoff
35 Rotterdam
36 Rouen
37 St. Malo
38 Strasbourg
39 Toulouse
40 Tours
41 Vlissingen Olau
42 Zeebrugge

Distance grid (each row lists the distances appearing on that line of the chart, followed by the diagonal city):

#	Distances (km)	City
1	159	Amsterdam
2	1298 1136	Antwerpen
3	408 246 1091	Biarritz
4	1093 931 199 887	Bordeaux
5	246 50 1097 892 239	Boulogne-sur-Mer
6	210 199 878 765 35 445	Brussel
7	643 481 786 581 305 204 445	Caen
8	373 211 1083 878 581 157 204 340	Calais
9	762 600 823 818 565 120 347 96 460	Cherbourg
10	925 763 581 371 561 425 319 723 561 710	Clermont-Ferrand
11	744 583 969 765 149 319 183 345 120 710 681	Dieppe
12	481 319 886 681 380 425 347 615 475 295 557 553	Dijon
13	326 164 1083 878 80 96 384 111 279 785 230 557 190	Dunkerque
14	1040 879 847 776 870 839 803 861 807 304 626 279 785 508	Grenoble
15	183 315 1454 1249 563 366 798 528 918 923 897 895 194 380 295	Groningen
16	64 132 1271 1066 380 345 345 615 626 785 638 729 380 194 496 203	Den Haag
17	582 420 890 685 244 380 111 347 96 507 279 475 291 730 138 138 307	Le Havre
18	243 119 1158 953 325 96 507 304 626 512 557 279 230 734 119 279 295 609	Liège
19	286 124 1011 806 114 117 356 114 475 626 451 451 96 648 194 295 380 156 203	Lille
20	896 734 427 222 690 695 451 729 230 239 475 379 615 525 525 638 485 473 490 203	Limoges
21	415 254 1155 950 429 213 615 419 734 648 729 293 293 796 329 335 329 73 242 554	Luxembourg
22	935 774 850 578 765 733 698 756 817 207 648 193 756 102 790 781 730 441 369 258 446	Lyon
23	712 550 636 432 376 511 110 497 207 442 279 475 484 625 387 295 156 369 247 295 554 307	Le Mans
24	1251 1090 719 648 1014 1072 974 1133 1049 315 911 315 1090 102 1049 978 911 754 841 470 473 156 609	Marseille
25	894 732 537 332 558 692 287 679 308 440 308 558 527 657 440 335 296 527 295 49 335 441 156 509	Nantes
26	1393 1245 877 806 1168 1227 1288 638 527 664 1128 440 1204 164 1146 1132 1000 816 881 473 881 242 992 203 992	Nice
27	283 121 1102 897 131 114 396 49 426 723 114 615 96 897 294 295 426 96 164 664 335 796 497 1227 567 1246	Oostende
28	641 479 666 461 383 240 277 293 360 164 361 313 383 666 416 360 295 387 293 239 397 613 164 974 280 881 383	Orleans
29	510 348 789 584 303 309 96 164 295 448 164 277 309 666 483 416 164 313 96 362 293 558 207 911 375 911 277 130	Paris
30	1380 1220 519 448 1179 1041 1202 1078 1103 445 1041 472 1055 273 1378 1121 816 521 613 349 501 354 483 204 499 66 1062 462 564	Perpignan
31	1063 901 769 564 383 240 331 361 203 667 361 594 396 881 1355 1132 296 816 483 836 975 966 232 1091 282 1153 383 376 497 717	Quimper
32	484 331 925 720 286 275 428 385 544 508 385 138 264 768 950 950 301 138 90 483 223 448 347 975 348 717 385 146 146 564 628	Reims
33	979 817 388 184 504 385 461 504 313 472 445 500 473 792 1235 1003 385 754 463 232 473 282 223 475 207 565 504 207 347 405 297 483	La Rochelle
34	911 867 662 653 764 778 444 588 347 919 475 768 504 933 1204 1092 385 892 564 836 959 799 297 1224 271 1191 504 470 470 778 146 799 459	Roscoff
35	92 100 1239 1034 278 275 651 461 567 930 375 596 278 1002 148 138 276 264 253 933 318 844 347 1002 334 1382 360 513 399 1321 1033 556 705 844	Rotterdam
36	518 356 824 619 370 385 62 446 89 546 89 499 426 922 872 777 62 475 215 522 447 643 135 953 207 834 422 138 138 953 317 283 271 384 479	Rouen
37	812 650 720 515 509 313 446 491 62 703 231 606 613 1091 1239 1034 347 703 491 565 611 930 179 1191 196 1278 565 355 355 1113 205 505 223 192 703 179	St. Malo
38	634 473 1269 1064 638 215 638 556 693 606 606 205 418 364 1504 1321 460 316 238 677 81 405 378 1432 565 1267 617 513 348 840 717 179 565 717 703 437 611	Strasbourg
39	1349 1187 314 243 902 937 671 840 702 316 784 486 902 272 1504 1321 607 636 719 206 536 332 355 179 271 687 807 399 399 237 611 437 205 717 1176 439 611 904	Toulouse
40	747 585 555 351 396 352 62 328 125 332 231 464 332 719 941 941 206 765 336 238 529 564 89 779 207 875 336 146 146 405 270 321 192 270 639 110 110 687 437	Tours
41	204 90 1126 921 532 617 532 590 752 941 545 902 360 1153 314 147 460 220 238 941 364 832 529 1148 540 1153 557 338 338 1209 875 890 819 875 345 607 611 1176 1153 345	Vlissingen Olau
42	265 101 1102 897 231 396 531 350 730 937 545 902 330 1321 585 297 559 321 309 832 551 775 516 1091 540 1246 285 332 332 1221 867 890 819 877 149 783 877 606 551 322 574	Zeebrugge

Map locations (as labelled):
Roscoff, Quimper, Cherbourg, Le Havre, St. Malo, Caen, Rouen, Dieppe, Boulogne, Calais, Dunkerque, Oostende, Zeebrugge, Vlissingen, Rotterdam, Den Haag, Amsterdam, Brussel, Antwerpen, Lille, Liège, Luxembourg, Reims, Paris, Orléans, Le Mans, Tours, Nantes, La Rochelle, Limoges, Bordeaux, Biarritz, Toulouse, Clermont-Ferrand, Dijon, Lyon, Strasbourg, Grenoble, Perpignan, Marseille, Nice